STREET NAMES
OF WIRRAL

BY
STEVEN HORTON

First Published 2003 by Countyvise Limited, 14 Appin Road, Birkenhead, Wirral CH41 9HH.

British Library Cataloguing in Publication Data.
A catalogue record for this book is available from the British Library.

ISBN 1 901231 40 2

For Lynne and Luke

Street Names Of Wirral

FOREWORD

Street names today are a great reminder of an area's past. Long gone farming communities, large houses and even campsites have been remembered in the streets of Wirral. As in many other areas of the country, members of the royalty, politicians and wartime heroes and events have streets named after them too. But this is less evident in Wirral, especially outside of Birkenhead and Wallasey.

In small villages the layout of streets has barely changed for over 100 years and the names reflect this. There are no streets named after famous people in Thurstaston for example, just the local church, station and school. But in the urbanised areas, developers have thrown up housing and reflected their literary tastes, favourite places or even political allegiances when naming streets. The Local Authority gives developers a free reign to name streets, but does ask them to try and avoid naming them after living persons.

There is a lot of debate as to what constitutes Wirral, but I have stuck with what is under the control of Wirral Metropolitan Borough Council. This follows on from my first book, in which I decided to concentrate on streets that lay solely within the Liverpool city boundary. This book does not aim to be analytical or a definitive guide to Wirral's street names, just a general overview that any reader can enjoy.

With Wirral being a collection of villages and towns that retain quite separate identities from each other there is a lot of overlap and duplication. Where this has occurred, I have not explained names in great detail more than once and the main explanation can be seen in the earlier chapter. In many instances this will be Birkenhead.

CONTENTS

BIRKENHEAD

There are two theories as to where the name Birkenhead comes from, both of which are connected with the headland. One possibility could be from the River Birket, the other may be from birch trees. The first known inhabitants were the Benedictine Monks of Birkenhead Priory. This was built around 1150 and for 400 years they and a few villagers were the only people who lived locally. When Henry VIII confiscated Church lands following the Dissolution of the Monasteries in the 1530s the local estates were given to Ralph Worsley.

Worsley has no streets named after him, but some of the other landowners who owned the Priory before it came into possession of the Town Council in 1824 have been remembered. John Cleveland, a Liverpool merchant and former MP bought the land in 1710 and is remembered today by **Cleveland Street**. When he died in 1716 it was inherited by his daughter Alice, who had married into the Price family, after whom **Price Street** is named.

Although four and a half centuries have passed, much of Birkenhead Priory is still standing and it is the oldest building on Merseyside. It has given rise to a number of street names in the surrounding area, with two obvious ones being **Priory Street** and **Priory Wharf**.

In 1820 the Prices paid for the construction of St Mary's Church, built next to the Priory. This was designed by Thomas Rickman and although it was demolished in 1975, its tower still stands and is open to the public. The church has given its name to **Church Street** and one of its earliest vicars, Reverend Andrew Knox, is remembered by **Knox Street**. He became the vicar in 1834 having first joined the church as a curate in 1828.

One of the main roles of the monks of Birkenhead Priory was to farm the land. Their nearest farm was at The Grange in Claughton. The modern roads of **Grange Road**, **Grange Mount** and **Grange Road West** led to this. But it was their other role for which the monks have left a greater legacy today. In 1330 Edward III granted the monks a charter to operate a ferry service across the River Mersey. The monks may have long gone but the ferry service has continued uninterrupted ever since, although the Mersey Tunnels means that most current passengers are pleasure cruisers rather than commuters.

Monks Ferry is named after the Monks Ferry Company that had been established in the 1830s. When this company was founded, it bought land around Ivy Rock House. At the time this was one of only a handful of notable houses in Birkenhead and has given its name to **Ivy Street**. Operations to Monks Ferry ceased in 1878 and today river cruises call at Woodside. This ferry link was developed in the 1820s and beat off competition due to its rail link. The Woodside ferry was also connected with the road to Chester by **Chester Street**.

Birkenhead remained the same size and with roughly the same population for many centuries before it grew after the arrival of William Laird in 1824. He came from a family of rope makers in Greenock and had moved to Liverpool in 1810. When he came to Birkenhead he bought some land around Wallasey Pool, on which he started an ironworks business with his eldest son John. In 1828 he began making ships, specialising in iron vessels and the business eventually went on to become the world famous Cammell Laird. William also saw the potential of building a new town almost from scratch, which he dubbed the 'city of the future'. He employed Edinburgh architect Gillespie Graham to design the town, with wide streets being laid out in a grid pattern. The scheme, which took two decades to complete, made Birkenhead one of the most advanced towns in Europe.

Hamilton Square was developed as the centrepiece of the new town. It remains one of the finest Georgian squares in the country, which was what Laird intended when it was developed. The square was named after Laird's mother, as was **Hamilton Street**, where the Town Hall and market hall were opened in 1835. The market has given its name to **Market Street**, while Laird didn't leave himself out when he named **Laird Street**. **Canning Street** was named after George Canning, a Liverpool MP who was Prime Minister for four months in 1824, dying whilst in office. One of the main streets, **Conway Street**, was developed by A.A. Dobbs. He named it after a relative, Conway Dobbs of Castle Dobbs in County Antrim.

When other streets were named, Laird's Scottish roots were not forgotten with some being influenced by his family and homeland. Duncan I was king of Scotland from 1034 to 1040 and was killed by Macbeth, one of his former generals, who was king of neighbouring Moray. Shakespeare's play Macbeth is based on this struggle between the two kings and **Duncan Street** was named in relation to Duncan. Another king of Scotland was Robert de Bruce, who reigned from 1306 to 1329. He fought several battles against the English with nobleman Sir William Douglas at his side. Douglas died in 1330 whilst taking Bruce's heart to be buried in the Holy Land and is remembered by **Douglas Street**.

In addition to streets named with a family and Scottish connection, Birkenhead's woodland history was remembered. Some local historians believe that the name Birkenhead means 'headland with the birches' and this is reflected by **Birchwood Avenue**, **Birchwood Close**, **Wood Street** and **Wood Close**. To the south of the town centre, Clifton Park, an estate of exclusive villas, was developed in the 1840s. This too was built on an area of previous woodland and can be seen in the street names there. On the northern perimeter of the estate is **The Woodlands**, with **Lowwood Road**, **Cedar Street** and **Maple Street** also being present nearby.

A pioneering development in Birkenhead was Birkenhead Park, the first municipally funded public park in the world. It opened in 1846 after being designed by Sir Joseph Paxton, head gardener to the Dukes of Devonshire. It contains five listed buildings and inspired many other parks throughout the world, including the famous Central Park in New York. The park is surrounded by **Park Road** (North, South, East and West), while to the north of the park the Duke of Devonshire's family name is remembered by **Cavendish Road** and **Cavendish Street**.

To the park's south, there is a **Devonshire Road**.

When Birkenhead fought for the right to build a docks system independent of Liverpool in the second quarter of the 19th century support had to be found in Parliament. One of the members of the Lords Committee that promoted it was Lord Ilchester, who is remembered by **Ilchester Road**. MP Sir Philip Egerton laid the foundation stone for the Great Float Dock System and one of the first two docks opened here in 1847 was named after him. This has given rise to the street of **Egerton Wharf**. These two docks were opened by Lord Morpeth, after whom **Morpeth Wharf** is named. He played a vital role in sorting out temporary entrances to the docks.

Around the same time as the docks, a bridge was built over Wallasey Pool connecting Birkenhead with Wallasey. This was built with wood and had a toll of ½d, which was raised to 1d in 1896. In 1926 it was replaced with a more modern bridge that is still in use today and sometimes known as the penny bridge. **Wallasey Bridge Road** is so named as it leads to the bridge.

In the 1870s Birkenhead became a borough with its own Mayor, and its boundaries were extended to include Claughton, Oxton and Tranmere. Lower Tranmere, at one time a fishing village that occupied the area between Holt Hill and the river, was once known as Hinderton and **Hinderton Road** remembers this. Birkenhead's new status was commemorated by one of the main roads built after the 1863 Improvement Act, **Borough Road**.

Another new road built around this time was the **New Chester Road**, which ran from Tranmere to Bromborough and allowed coaches to travel from Birkenhead to Chester without passing through villages. This new route meant that the original turnpike road became known as the **Old Chester Road**. Thomas Brassey, developer of the new road, would develop transport links far beyond Birkenhead. Born in Buerton in 1805, he came to Birkenhead at the age of 21 to work for a land agent. He then set up on his own and went on to become a successful railway contractor, building lines all over the world, including the Grand Trunk Railway in Canada. **Brassey Street** and **Upper Brassey Street** are both named after him.

As Birkenhead grew at a rapid pace in the second quarter of the 19th century, it soon became quite apparent that St Mary's Church would not be sufficient to serve the town's ever expanding population. A number of new churches were built, many of which still stand today. Some of these, as well as ones that have since been demolished have given their name to streets throughout the town.

The first Catholic church, St Werburghs, was built in 1834. This is still standing today and retains its old burial ground. **St Werburghs Square** is named after the church, which was named after St Werburghs Abbey, the name for Chester Cathedral prior to 1541.

Holy Trinity Church was built in 1837 and has been remembered by **Trinity Street**. The tower measured 82 feet and the churches first vicar was Reverend Joseph Baylee. He established St Aidans Theological College off Shrewsbury Road, which has given its name to **St Aidans Court**. Near to here is **St Stephens Road**, named after St Stephens Church. The church's vicarage has given rise to the name of **Vicarage Close**.

St Johns Church, which was built in 1845, is no longer in existence. However, **St Johns Street** and **St Johns Square** remain as a reminder of it. The construction of the church was funded by John Somerville Jackson, William Jackson and also Joseph Mallaby, who is commemorated by **Mallaby Street**. Mallaby was involved in the legal profession and his business partner gave his name to **Townsend Street**.

Still in existence is St Annes Church, which has been near the corner of **St Anne Street** and Duke Street since 1847. This was built in 1847 with sandstone from the Claughton quarries by William Potter. It has also given its name to **St Annes Grove**, **St Annes Place** and **St**

Annes Way. Another church built that year at Potter's expense and using sandstone from Claughton was Christ Church, off Bessborough Road. This has been remembered by **Christchurch Road**.

At the western end of Laird Street is St James Church, of which the Lairds were a benefactor. **St James Road** takes its name from the church, which is situated where a number of main roads converge. One of these is **Sumner Road**, which was named after Dr John Bird Sumner, who became Bishop of Chester in 1828.

As Birkenhead grew, streets were named after military events, politicians and royalty, keeping in line with other towns and cities in England. **Waterloo Place** is named after the Battle of Waterloo (1815), when the Duke of Wellington defeated the French. This brought the Napoleonic wars, a series of conflicts that had raged for sixteen years, to an end. **Vittoria Street** was named after the Battle of Vittoria that took place in northern Spain in 1813, the first step in driving Napoleon out of the Iberian peninsular.

John Somerville Jackson owned land in central Birkenhead around what is now the Pyramid Shopping Centre and laid out a number of streets named after military events. Some of these are now long gone but two have survived in a shortened form. **Horatio Street** remembers Horatio Nelson, naval hero of the Napoleonic Wars and **St Vincent Street** commemorates a victory in which he took part off Cape St Vincent, Portugal in 1797.

A year after the Napoleonic Wars ended a British and Dutch naval expedition attacked the city of Algiers in North Africa. This was in response to a number of acts of piracy that it had committed in the Mediterranean. The Algerian fleet was nearly all destroyed and one of the British commanders, Exmouth is remembered by **Exmouth Street**.

A later war was fought in the Crimea from 1853 to 1856 between Britain, France and Turkey on one side and Russia on the other. This was for control of the straits between the Mediterranean and Black Seas and **Alma Street** is named after the Battle of Alma, when coalition forces gained control of the River Alma.

The war that seems to have most streets named after it in Birkenhead is the Boer War. This took place from 1899 to 1902 between Britain and the Boers, descendants of Dutch settlers in South Africa. The streets in question are all situated between Corporation Road and Laird Street.

Plumer Street is named after Colonel Hubert Plumer, who masterminded the Relief of Mafeking in May 1900, after it had been under siege for 217 days. Another siege was at Ladysmith, which lasted for four months until March 1900 and was ended by cavalry leader Lord Dundonald. He is remembered by **Dundonald Street**. Lord Methuen, after whom **Methuen Street** is named, was a commander who was wounded and taken prisoner in 1901. After the war he was Commander of the British Army in South Africa and Governor of Natal.

Major General Sir Leslie Rundle commanded the 8th Division during the Boer War, having taken part in a number of earlier African campaigns. He gives his name to **Rundle Street**. A volunteer force during the campaigns was Thorneycroft's Mounted Infantry, after whom **Thorneycroft Street** is named. One of the most important posts at home during the Boer War was Chairman of the Inland Revenue, which was held by Alfred Milner. His success in this role led to him being made a viscount and appointed as Governor of Transvaal after the war ended. He is remembered by **Milner Street**, which completes the set of Boer War streets.

Off Church Road near Mersey Park, the English Civil War, which was fought between parliamentary and royalist forces from 1642 to 1648, has been commemorated centuries after it happened. **Hampden Road** is named after John Hampden whose refusal to pay a ship tax led to his imprisonment and the outbreak of hostilities. **Fairfax Road** remembers Thomas Fairfax, commander in chief of the Parliamentary army.

Around Park Road North, Conway Street and Claughton Road, a number of streets have been named after politicians of the Victorian period. These include **Aberdeen Street**, which was named after George Hamilton Gordon, 4th Earl of Aberdeen, who was Prime Minister from 1852 to 1855. He led Britain into the Crimean War but resigned due to the fact it was not going too well. He was succeeded as Prime Minister by Henry John Temple, 3rd Viscount Palmerston, who held the post for nine of the next ten years and gives his name to **Palmerston Street**. Another Prime Minister who led the country during wartime was Herbert Asquith, who was in office before and during World War 1. **Asquith Avenue** is named after him.

Next to these streets is **Livingstone Street**. This is named after the Scottish missionary Dr. David Livingstone, who spent half his life exploring Africa. In 1858 he visited Birkenhead to supervise the stowing of his paddle boat Ma Robert, which was used for his expedition up the Zambezi River.

William Gladstone was born in Liverpool in 1809 and has the unique distinction of having four separate spells as Prime Minister between 1868 and 1894. He gives his name to **Gladstone Close**. During his first two administrations, the Marquis of Hartington, after whom **Hartington Avenue** is named, was his Postmaster General and India Secretary. Sir William Harcourt was a novice MP when Gladstone first became Prime Minister, but was Home Secretary in his second spell from 1880 to 1885. Then during Gladstone's third and fourth terms in office in 1886 and from 1892 to 1894, he served as Chancellor of the Exchequer. After Gladstone's retirement he led the Liberal Party until 1898 and was disappointed never to be Prime Minister. **Harcourt Street** is named after him.

With Birkenhead growing so quickly when Queen Victoria was on the throne (1837-1901), it is natural that she and her family were honoured by some street names.

Victoria became Queen on the death of her uncle, William IV in 1837. His wife, Adelaide of Saxe-Meiningen died in 1849 and was remembered by **Adelaide Road**, near the southern end of Borough Road. Next to this is **Albert Road**, named after Victoria's husband, Albert of Saxe Coburg Gotha. In the same vicinity is **Victoria Road**, while Albert is also remembered in central Birkenhead by **Coburg Street**. Off Laird Street and Park Road North, three streets remember Prince Arthur, Duke of Connaught, who was Victoria's third son. He was a career soldier who served in South Africa and India and **Arthur Street**, **Connaught Close** and **Connaught Way** are named after him.

Victoria Park was opened in 1901, the year Victoria died. It was originally the gardens of Arudy House, owned by French cotton merchant Victor Poutz. The park has given its name to **Victoria Park Road**, while **Albany Road**, which runs alongside it, is name after her fourth and youngest son Leopold, Duke of Albany. South of Victoria Park, off Bebington Road, is **Alexandra Drive**, named after Alexandra, daughter of Christian IX of Denmark. She married the heir to the throne Prince Albert Edward in 1863 and on the death of his mother he became Edward VII.

Near to Ilchester Road are a number of streets named after rivers. This is in relation to a major scheme begun before World War 1 to upgrade Birkenhead's water supply, when the Corporation looked to pipe water in from North Wales. This project was completed in 1921, with water now being drawn from the Alwen reservoir in Clwyd, created from the damming of a river of the same name. **Alwen Street** commemorates this, whilst another Welsh river gives its name to **Brenig Street**. Also present are **Humber Street**, **Ribble Street**, **Severn Street**, **Tees Street**, **Trent Street** and **Tyne Street**, which are named after English rivers. Scotland has not been forgotten, with **Solway Street** and **Tweed Street** taking their names from rivers north of the border. Finally, an Irish river is remembered by **Shannon Street**. Prior to the development of the Alwen Reservoir, water in Birkenhead had been supplied from various local pumps and reservoirs. For example, Prenton Reservoir stood at the bottom of **Reservoir Road**.

The development of Birkenhead to incorporate surrounding areas such as Rock Ferry had been inevitable since the first steam powered ferry had crossed the Mersey in 1817. This ferry, the Etna, is commemorated by **Etna Street** in Rock Ferry. The introduction of a steam service meant that the Mersey crossing was now reliable. Previously it could take up to half a day to cross dependent on the weather conditions.

With a fast ferry connection to Liverpool, Rock Ferry became a very popular place to live. There were no more desirable residences than in the Rock Park estate, which was built in the 1830s and 1840s to the design of Jonathan Bennison. The most famous resident was American author Nathaniel Hawthorne, who was US Consul to Liverpool from 1853 to 1857. However most of these properties, including Hawthorne's home at number 26, were demolished in the 1970s for the creation of the New Ferry bypass. The estates name has lived on in **Rock Park** and **Rock Park Road**.

When the Rock Park estate was completed in 1850, the Prime Minister was Lord John Russell. Nearby, off New Chester Road are some streets to commemorate this and the most obvious is **Russell Road**. Russell was the third son of the 6th Duke of Bedford, who was a supporter of parliamentary reform in the early 19th century. This gives rise to **Bedford Road**. The Bedford's seat was at Woburn Abbey in Bedfordshire, hence the name **Woburn Place**. St Peters Church was consecrated in 1842 to meet local religious demand. It was built to a Norman design and gives its name to **St Peters Road**.

A small group of streets off the Old Chester Road, near Mersey Park, have also been named after politicians of the 19th century. One of these is **Peel Avenue**, which remembers Sir Robert Peel, founder of the modern Conservative Party and Prime Minister from 1834 to 1835 and 1841 to 1846. Earlier, as Home Secretary, he had been responsible for the formation of the Metropolitan Police in 1829. **Brougham Avenue** is named after Henry Peter Brougham, 1st Baron Brougham. He was Lord Chancellor from 1830 to 1834, having been elected to Parliament as a Liberal in 1810.

14

Beaconsfield Close remembers Benjamin Disraeli, the Earl of Beaconsfield. As an MP in the 1840s he was also a successful novelist, then went on to become Chancellor of the Exchequer in the 1850s and Prime Minister in 1868 and from 1874 to 1880. **Cobden Avenue** and **Cobden Place** are named after Victorian economist and statesman Richard Cobden, who was very active in the promotion of free trade.

As Birkenhead tentacles expanded further in the 20th century, many of the Victorian villas of Rock Ferry were demolished by developers to make way for new housing. Those that have been remembered in street names include **Hurst Bank**, **Stoneleigh Grove**, **Woodcote Bank**, **Woodland Road** and **Woodland Grove**. One building that has survived as part of Rock Ferry High School is Ravenswood, which is also remembered by **Ravenswood Avenue**.

One of the themes the new developers used to name streets was literature, with many streets near to Rock Ferry station being named after poets and authors. The most obvious is **Shakespeare Avenue**, named after William Shakespeare (1564-1616). He was England's greatest ever playwright and used poetry to express human feelings. **Spenser Avenue** is named after another Elizabethan poet, Edmund Spenser (1554-99). His most famous work was *The Faerie Queene*, of which only six of the intended twelve books were completed.

Also in this vicinity is **Ruskin Avenue**, which remembers Victorian writer and art critic John Ruskin (1819-1900). Another street with a literary theme from this era is **Browning Avenue**, named after Robert Browning (1812-89), writer of the *Pied Piper of Hamlin*. However neither Ruskin nor Browning were as influential in their day as Lord Alfred Tennyson (1809-92), who gives his name to **Tennyson Avenue**. He wrote in a number of different styles and was appointed Poet Laureate in 1850 and made a peer in 1884.

Wordsworth Avenue was named after William Wordsworth (1770-1850), who preceded Tennyson as Poet Laureate. Considered by many to be England's most influential ever poet, he was inspired by the beautiful scenery of his Lake District surroundings. Another Poet Laureate was Rudyard Kipling (1865-1936), who is remembered by **Kipling Avenue**. He wrote a number of poems, short stories and novels that were set in India and Myanmar under British colonial rule, of which *The Jungle Book* is perhaps the most famous. Finally, **Bulwer Street** and **Lytton Avenue** were named after Edward George Bulwer Lytton (1803-73), whose novels included Pelham in 1828 and The Last Days of Pompeii in 1834. He later went on to enjoy a political career and was appointed Colonial Secretary in 1858.

A literary themed street that stands alone and is not part of any cluster of similarly named streets is **Wilfred Owen Drive** in Claughton. Born in Oswestry in 1893, his family lived in Elm Grove from 1897 to 1906 and he attended Birkenhead Institute. An Officer in World War 1, he wrote a number of poems describing the horrors of battle and was killed just one week before hostilities ceased in November 1918. An English Heritage Blue Plaque is situated on the wall of the house where he lived.

William Jackson, who was Lord of the Manor of Claughton in the 1840s, built a residence called the Manor House. The Italianate building had twenty bedrooms and was set in ten acres of land, but was demolished to make way for the current houses that stand on **Manor Hill**. Another major landowner in Claughton during the mid 19th century was James Ball, who purchased a lot of land in 1836. He is remembered by **Balls Road** and **Balls Road East**. Robert Vyner, who owned much of neighbouring Bidston in the 19th century, lived in Gautby, Lincolnshire, which is reflected in **Gautby Road**. One of Birkenhead's MPs in the 19th century, John Tollemache, is remembered by **Tollemache Road**.

In Oxton the Earls of Shrewsbury owned a lot of land and have given their name to a small number of streets there, including **Shrewsbury Road**. In addition **Chetwynd Road** and **Talbot Road** are named after the family surname of Chetwynd-Talbot, while former Staffordshire homes are remembered by **Alton Road** and **Ingestre Road**. Alton Towers was their main home until 1924 and is now a major leisure attraction, while Ingestre Hall was sold in 1960 and is now an education centre. Connecting Ingestre Road and Talbot Road is **Mill Hill**, which was named after an old peg mill that stood at its top and was destroyed around 1850.

Normanston Road and **Normanston Close** take their names from a house called Normanston that was built in the 1860s by Butler Gasquoine. He lived there for ten years and it was later converted to flats in the 1930s.

Just south of Storeton Road two streets are named after politicians. **Rosebery Grove** is named after the Earl of Rosebery, who was Prime Minister from 1894 to 1895. He had succeeded Gladstone, whom he had served as Foreign Secretary from 1892 to 1894. Another street here is **Curzon Road**, which takes its name from George Curzon, who served as Viceroy of India and then Foreign Secretary from 1919 to 1924.

Nearby, Prenton is rare in that it contains some streets named in relation to the reigning Queen, Elizabeth II. **Queen's Drive** is named after Elizabeth, while **Edinburgh Drive** takes its name from her husband, Prince Philip, Duke of Edinburgh. **Cornwall Drive** commemorates the title of Duke of Cornwall, which Prince Charles took when his mother became Queen in 1952.

Prenton Hall Road is named after Prenton Hall Farm. This was built in the 17th century on the site of Prenton Hall, which had been mentioned in the Domesday Book during the 11th century. The land was sold after World War 2 for a housing development and the farm has been remembered by **Prenton Farm Road**. Prenton Waterworks were erected in the 1860s and were reached by a track that is now **Waterpark Road**. **Duck Pond Lane** was once known as the 'cinder path'. It is named after a man made pond that is now covered by a car park and was once part of a poultry farm where ducks were kept.

Between Prenton Dell Road and Prenton Village Road, some writers have been honoured. **Dickens Avenue** and **Dickens Close** remember the great Victorian novelist Charles Dickens, but some literary figures of the previous century have also had streets named after them. One of these is James Boswell, who gives his name to **Boswell Road**. He was a Scottish lawyer whose travels in Europe prompted him to write *An Account of Corsica* in 1768, devoted to the island's struggle for independence.

In 1791 Boswell wrote the biography *Life of Samuel Johnson*, in remembrance of his friend, poet Samuel Johnson who died in 1784. **Johnson Road** is named after him, while two other members of their literary circle are remembered by **Garrick Road** and **Goldsmith Road**. David Garrick was an actor and playwright who once attended a school run by Johnson, while Oliver Goldsmith was a friend who Johnson saved from jail. Famed for spending more than he earned, he faced a debtor's prison in 1766 before Johnson hastily arranged for the publication of *The Vicar of Wakefield* to bring in some much needed funds.

The world's highest mountain, Everest was first conquered by Edmund Hilary in 1953, but 29 years earlier two Birkenhead men, George Mallory and Sandy Irvine, both died trying to make it to the summit. Mallory's body was only discovered in 1999 and Irvine's is still somewhere on the mountain. There remains considerable debate as to whether the two climbers died on their way to the top or coming back down after having reached there. If Irvine's body is ever found, a camera he was carrying may give the final answer as to whether or not they did indeed make the summit. On either side of Borough Road near to Tranmere Rovers football ground, a number of streets are named after mountains big and small to commemorate two of Birkenhead's most famous sons.

The two climbers themselves are remembered by **Mallory Road** and **Irvine Road**, while the mountain that claimed their lives gives its name to **Everest Road**. The highest mountains of Wales and Scotland are represented by **Ben Nevis Road** and **Snowdon Road**. However these two peaks, standing at 4,406 and 3,560 feet respectively, would have presented little challenge to Mallory compared to Everest, which towers at 29,028 feet. **Ingleborough Road** is named after one of England's highest points, Ingleborough Peak in Yorkshire, which is a relatively small 2,373 feet.

It is not just individual mountains that are named, as some of the streets here have been named after British ranges. The Cheviot Hills separate England and Scotland and have been the scene of many border skirmishes in bygone days. Their highest point is 2,676 feet and they have given their name to **Cheviot Road**. **Pennine Road** is named after the Pennines, which separate Lancashire and Yorkshire and are nearly as high as 3,000 feet in places.

As well as these northern ranges, southern ones are remembered too, although hills would be a better way of describing them than mountains. **Malvern Grove** is named after the Malvern Hills that separate Herefordshire and Worcestershire. The Cotswold Hills in Gloucestershire, which have a high point of just 1,031 feet, give their name to **Cotswold Road**. The Chiltern Hills north west of London have an even smaller peak of 852 feet, but are commemorated by **Chiltern Road**. Another small range that has given their name to a street are the Mendip Hills, which separate Gloucestershire from Avon. **Mendip Road** is named after them. Finally, **Brecon Road** takes its name from the Brecon Beacons in South Wales.

As Birenhead looks to the future and Cammell Laird has moved from ship building to repairing, some streets do remember some of the vessels that have been built there. The Ark Royal was commissioned in 1955 and at the time was the largest aircraft carrier in the world at 43,000 tonnes, remaining in service until 1978 when it was replaced by another vessel of the same name that was built in Newcastle. An earlier version of the Ark Royal had been built at the yard in 1937 and was the UK's first purpose built aircraft carrier. It was sunk off Gibraltar in 1941 and **Ark Royal Way** has been named after them.

The last vessel to be built at Cammell Laird was the nuclear submarine HMS Unicorn in 1993. This has given its name to **Unicorn Way**. A ship built very early on in Cammell Laird's history was the CSS Alabama. This was used as a Confederate raider in the American Civil War, although it was ordered by a private individual acting as an agent as it would have been illegal to deal direct with the Confederate government. The ship was so successful that Anglo-American relations at the time were strained, but it has still been remembered today by **Alabama Way**.

BEBINGTON, PORT SUNLIGHT AND BROMBOROUGH

200 years ago Bebington was a small hamlet of less than 300 people that was a popular stopping point for stagecoaches travelling along the Old Chester Road. The opening of the New Chester Road in the mid 19th century reduced this traffic, making it an attractive backwater for Liverpool businessmen seeking a quiet place to live. This meant that the population had risen to over 3,000 by the end of the century.

By far the most influential figure in the development of Bebington was Joseph Mayer, after whom **Mayer Avenue** is named. A Staffordshire born merchant, he retired to Bebington in 1864 after working in Liverpool. He built a free library and museum, stockpiling them with his own books, paintings and sculptures. The building that housed these, Mayer Hall is still in use for community events, having ceased to be used for council business when the Civic Centre was built in 1971. He also donated a small park, which stands behind these buildings in five acres of land, giving rise to **Parkside Road**.

Mayer is buried in the graveyard of St Andrews Church, which has given its name to **Church Road** and **St Andrews Road**. This church dates from Norman times and is built on the site of an earlier Saxon place of worship. Leading to the church from the west is **Kirket Lane**, kirk being a Norman word for church. It was once occupied by young monks who were training for priesthood and there have been a number of ghostly sightings in the area. Whether these were real apparitions or figments of imagination depends on one's belief in ghosts, but there is no doubt that some local streets have been named in relation to the monks. They are **Abbots Drive**, **Friars Close** and **Monks Way**.

An old house in Bebington that is remembered by a modern road is Larchwood, after which **Larchwood Drive** is named. **Rocklands**

21

Avenue is named after a house of the same name that stood at the end of the road near the railway line. This house was so called as a quarry was once situated at its junction with Old Chester Road. Another street named after a house is **Oaklands Drive**.

There are two small groups of streets in Bebington named after events and figures from the Napoleonic Wars. Off Bromborough Road near Port Sunlight station a small hamlet called Trafalgar developed, named in relation to the Battle of Trafalgar in 1805. This naval battle, fought off the coast of southern Spain, gave British coalition forces control of the seas for the rest of the campaigns. The British forces were led by Admiral Lord Nelson, who was killed in the battle. He is not remembered by any streets here but his deputy, Admiral Lord Collingwood, is commemorated by **Collingwood Road**. He took over command of the fleet for the rest of the battle after Nelson's death, having earlier kept the enemy at bay for more than an hour before the main fleet arrived. The battle itself is remembered by **Trafalgar Drive**, while **Erfurt Avenue** is named after the 1808 Erfurt Convention. At this meeting in Germany Napoleon tried to offer peace to Britain in return for recognition of his control of Spain.

The other streets named after the Napoleonic Wars are near to where Bebington Road meets Old Chester Road. **Wellesley Grove**, **Wellington Road** and **Wellington Close** remember Arthur Wellesley, the Duke of Wellington, who led the coalition forces at the Battle of Waterloo. Wellington later served as Prime Minister between 1828 and 1830 and lived at Apsley House, which was described by Queen Victoria in her diaries as one of the four finest houses in London. In Bebington it is commemorated by **Apsley Grove**. Another to be remembered here is William Carr Beresford, after whom **Beresford Avenue** is named. Despite being captured at Buenos Aries in 1806, Beresford was always held in high regard by Wellington who wanted him to take his place if anything ever happened to him. After being put in charge of the Portuguese army he was wounded at Salamanca in 1812 and later held government positions when Wellington was Prime Minister.

A number of streets with Shakespearean connections are situated in the Woodhey area off Town Lane. Beatrice, a character who appeared in two of his plays, *As You Like It* and *Twelfth Night*, gives her name to **Beatrice Avenue**. **Cressida Avenue** is named after one of the two lovers in the play *Troilus and Cressida*, which was based on a medieval legend. Other female lovers to be remembered are Juliet, who is a title character of *Romeo and Juliet* and after whom **Juliet Avenue** is named, as well as Miranda, who features in *The Tempest* and gives her name to **Miranda Avenue**. **Rosalind Avenue** is named after a character from *As You Like It* who tries to come between two lovers and **Portia Avenue** remembers a character from *The Merchant of Venice*.

The name of New Ferry comes about from a ferry service that was begun in 1865 by Robert MacFie, who constructed an iron pier here. The service was taken over by Birkenhead Corporation at the end of the 19th century, but soon went into decline after the onset of an electric tramcar route connecting the area with Woodside. The New Ferry closed in 1922, but not before it had become swamped by southern expansion of Birkenhead. In New Ferry two Cheshire MPs from the mid 19th century gave their names to **Legh Road** and **Egerton Road**.

Off New Chester Road, near New Ferry Park, some poets of old and modern times have been remembered by four cul-de-sacs that run off **Longfellow Drive**. This is named after an American, Henry Wadsworth Longfellow (1807-82), whose poetry was inspired by his interest in mythology and travels around Europe. Another American, T.S.Eliot (1888-1965) is remembered by **Eliot Close**. One of his most famous works was the 1936 collection *Old Possum's Book of Practical Cats*, which inspired Sir Andrew Lloyd Webber's stage musical *Cats*. Although he won the Nobel Prize in 1948, Eliot said that his creativity wasn't worth the personal suffering it had caused him.

British poets have not been forgotten in this small group of streets, with **Coleridge Drive** being named after Samuel Taylor Coleridge (1772-1834). The son of a Devon vicar, he developed an interest in

23

radical politics whilst at Cambridge University and went on to write an anti war poem, *Fire, Famine and Slaughter*. In 1797 he met William Wordsworth and with him published *Lyrical Ballads*, which was deemed by many critics a literary revolution because of its new style.

John Masefield (1878-1967), who was Poet Laureate from 1930 to 1967, is remembered by **Masefield Close**. As a sea cadet, he spent time on the training ship HMS Conway, which was anchored on the River Mersey. His 1902 book *Salt Water Ballads* contains more poems commemorating events on Merseyside than any other. **Larkin Close** is named after Philip Larkin (1922-85). Unable to serve in World War 2 because of poor eyesight, he studied English at Oxford University and had some poems published in *Oxford Poetry* and *Poetry From Oxford in Wartime*. He went on to combine poetry with a career as a librarian, receiving many literary awards as well as the CBE in 1975. In 1984 he turned down the opportunity to become Poet Laureate because he didn't want a high public profile or any media intrusion into his life. However, he died just a year later of throat cancer.

In 1888, William Hesketh Lever began to build Port Sunlight, a village that would not only house his soap factory but the workforce as well. Initially just 28 houses were built but by 1900 this had grown to over 400. When the decision was made to extend the village further in 1910, a competition was held, which was won by Liverpool University architecture student Ernest Prestwich. This increased the number of houses to 800 and the population to 4,000. The village, which had its own school, technical institute and art gallery, was held up as a prime example of future living. One of the main features of the village was the differing architectural styles, as no two rows of houses are the same design. It is still intact today and is a designated conservation area.

The village was bounded by the railway, Wood Street, New Chester Road and Bebington Road. The first street to be built was **Bolton Road**, which was named after the Lancashire town of Bolton, where Lever was born in 1851. Another main road was **Corniche Road**, which is another word for boulevard. Christ Church, which was opened in 1904, gave its name to **Church Drive**. The hospital was built in 1907 and had room for fourteen patients in two wards. There were also residential quarters for a doctor and **Hospital Road** has been named after it. **Poet's Corner** is a small street with a name deriving from a block of cottages, now demolished, that were a reproduction of Willam Shakespeare's birthplace in Stratford upon Avon.

The factory had been built because Lever's business had outgrown its previous home, Percy Winser's chemical works in Warrington. This had been leased since 1885 and is remembered in Port Sunlight by **Winser Street**. Male workers in the factory ate their meals at Gladstone Hall, which was opened in 1891 by William Gladstone. By 1910 it was too small, despite accommodating 800 and workers transferred to a new canteen inside the factory. But the high vaulted building has always remained in use, mainly as a theatre and **Gladstone Hall Road** is named after it. **Water Street** and **Wharf Street** were named due to their proximity to Bromborough Pool.

Three monarchs who reigned during Port Sunlight's development are all commemorated. **Victoria Street** remembers Queen Victoria, while her son Edward VII gives his name to **King Edward Drive**. His son, George V visited the village in 1914 with Queen Mary. They doubted that the cottages could be as nice inside as outside but where proved wrong when they were shown around one. **King George's Drive** and **Queen Mary's Drive** are named after them, while around the same time **The Causeway** was developed. This was a wide boulevard leading to the Lady Lever Art Gallery, which was built between 1913 and 1922. The last houses to be built in Port Sunlight were in 1938 in **Jubilee Crescent**, which was named as it was the 50th anniversary of the village.

Early in the 20th century the development of Port Sunlight had been continued across New Chester Road with the Bromborough Port and Woodhead estates. These remained separate from the village proper and the part circular **Corona Road** was named after the Latin name for a circle.

25

East of Port Sunlight is the small village of Bromborough Pool, which was built thirty years before Lever's scheme to house workers of Price's candle factory. A total of 147 houses were built, with the oldest street being **York Street**. This was named after York Road in Battersea, where the company's first factory had been established. The company had decided to establish a base near the port of Liverpool to cut down on the cost of transporting imported palm oil that was required for production. **The Green** was named after the bowling green that stood next to where the village's cricket club was established, while **Pool Lane** leads to the village. It is still known as Price's Village today despite the candle factory being taken over by Unilever in 1937.

Bromborough dates from Norse or Saxon times and development grew at a pace after World War 1. Most traces of the ancient past have gone, but central Bromborough still retains a village feel and has old names such as **The Rake** and **Bromborough Village Road**. Bromborough Cross, the base of which may date from the 13th century, stands in the centre of the village. This is an old market cross, one of very few left in England today. They marked the location of the main trading area of a town or village and this is reflected by **High Street**. **Old Hall Road** remembers Bromborough Hall, an early 17th century building that stood near the church and was demolished in 1932.

In the mid 19th century the Lord of the Manor was Salisbury Kynaston Mainwaring and he is remembered by **Mainwaring Road**. **Brotherton Close** is named after another landowner, Lord Brotherton, who made the gift of Brotherton Park. Thomas Forwood, who once lived at Thornton Manor is commemorated by **Forwood Road**. In Poulton, **Venables Drive** and **Venables Close** are named after a Norman landowner, Gilbert de Venables.

When the area of Liscard that used to store gunpowder from ships entering Liverpool became too populated in the 1850s, an offshore site at Bromborough was chosen. Three wooden hulks were moored in the Mersey and the area onshore became known as Magazines Village, as some houses were built there to accommodate workers. The hulks remained in use until just after World War 2 and have given rise to the name of **Magazine Road**.

A very old building in Bromborough is Stanhope House, which was built in 1693. For many years it served as a library but is now in private ownership. **Stanhope Drive** is named after the house, which stands at the corner of Mark Rake and Spital Road. **Mark Rake** is named in relation to marks that are situated in the walls of the house, which predate it. These marks were probably made by archers sharpening their arrows.

Bromborough Golf Club has given rise to a number of streets named after golf courses from around the country. Although not as famous as the Royal Liverpool Golf Club at Hoylake, Bromborough Golf Club is none the less an excellent and well respected course. It was founded in 1904 by Mr J. Hassall and despite losing land to the World War 2 effort and then construction of the M53, it bounced back in the early 1970s when Lord Leverhulme made some farmland available to the course. The reconstructed course then hosted the County Championships in 1975. The streets that are named after golf courses are situated off Brookhurst Avenue.

Ainsdale Close is named after the Southport and Ainsdale Golf Club, which hosted the Ryder Cup match between Britain and America in 1933. Another Southport course is Royal Birkdale, which has hosted eight Open championships and gives its name to **Birkdale Drive**.

It is not just Merseyside courses that are commemorated in Bromborough. **Sunningdale Drive** is named after Sunningdale Golf Club in Berkshire, which hosted the European Open in 1982, while Fairhaven Golf Club in Lancashire is remembered by **Fairhaven Drive**. **Wentworth Drive** is named after Surrey's Wentworth Golf Club, home of the biennial World Match Play Championships. Finally, Royal Troon Golf Club in Ayrshire, which has staged seven Open championships, gives its name to **Troon Close**.

Eastham dates from Norman times and remained in the hands of the Stanley family from the 16th century to the mid 19th century, hence **Stanley Lane**. Dibbinsdale Brook flows through Eastham and **Brookhurst Avenue** takes its name from this. **Ferry Road** connects Eastham Village with Eastham Ferry, which was in operation until 1928. The iron pier that had been built in 1874 was demolished seven years later.

BIDSTON, UPTON & WOODCHURCH

Sandwiched between Birkenhead and Moreton, the ancient sandstone village of Bidston has struggled to maintain an identity amidst the progress of urban development. Prior to the 1970s there were considerable traffic problems but these were resolved by the construction of the bypass.

A rural character remains in **Bidston Village Road**, the main road through the village. Bidston's church, St Oswald's, has given its name to **St Oswald's Avenue**. The current building was built in 1856, retaining an earlier tower from 1520. However, there has been a church on the site since the 12th century. **School Lane** is named as it led to the Old School House, which was built in 1636 at the cost of £200 on land donated by James Stanley. This was replaced by a new school in Bidston Village Road in 1838. This new school was destroyed by a German air raid in 1941.

Most of the land in Bidston was bought by banker and goldsmith Sir Robert Vyner in the late 17th century. He and his descendants were largely absentee landlords, selling land bit by bit for development until their last holding Bidston Hall was sold in 1969 to architect Maxwell Faulkner. The family have been honoured by **Vyner Road North**, **Vyner Road South** and **Vyner Close**, while **Eleanor Road** is named after the wife of Henry Vyner, who inherited the land in 1872.

An example of a piecemeal sale of land occurred in 1866 when they sold the land on which Bidston Observatory was built. This had been built by the Mersey Docks and Harbour Board so that ships using the port of Liverpool could set their chronometers accurately. In 1929 its work switched to monitoring tides and it retains this function today. **Observatory Road** is named after it.

Off Eleanor Road, some streets have been named after famous cricket grounds and players. **Lords Avenue** and **Edgbaston Way** are named after the test venues of Lords and Edgbaston, situated in London and Birmingham respectively. **Cowdrey Avenue** commemorates Colin Cowdrey (1933-2000). He is England's fourth highest scoring test cricketer and in 1997 was appointed to the House of Lords. **Trueman Close** remembers Fred Trueman, the former England and Yorkshire fast bowler who is still alive today. Jack Ikin (1918-84), a Lancashire and England batsman, gives his name to **Ikin Close**.

Staying with the cricketing theme Lancashire's youngest batsman to score a century was Cyril Washbrook (1918-99), who achieved the feat aged eighteen in 1933. He went on to enjoy a test career that spanned twenty years and **Washbrook Avenue** is named after him. **Lillie Close** is named after Australian Dennis Lillie (born 1945), who jointly holds the record for reaching 200 wickets in the least number of tests. Another Australian, pace bowler Ray Lindwall (1921-96) is remembered by **Lindwall Close**. All these cul-de-sacs are off **Statham Road**, which is named after Brian Statham (1930-2000). He took more wickets for Lancashire than any other bowler and in 1966 was awarded the CBE, the first bowler to be recognised in the Honours List.

The southern part of Bidston is now taken up by housing developments. They were once farmland and this is reflected in street names such as **Broadfield Avenue** and **Farmfield Drive**.

In the 19th century Upton gained in importance due to its position at the junction of roads connecting a number of neighbouring villages, its population rising from 141 to 788.

William Inman, founder of the Inman Line which specialised in taking emigrants to America on steamships, came to live in Upton Hall in 1855. He then built a new home, Upton Manor in 1857 and in 1868 he donated the land and paid for 75% of the cost of building St Mary's Church. Inman remained Lord of the Manor of Upton till he died in 1881 and is remembered by **Inman Road**, while **Church Road** is named after the church he helped pay for. His home, which was initially named Harefield House, has given its name to **Manor Drive**.

Upton Hall and Upton Manor are both still in existence today and are grade II listed buildings, the former being a girl's school and the latter a nursing home. However, they are the only two of eight large houses that existed in Upton at the beginning of the 20th century that are still standing.

One of those houses no longer in existence is The Salacres. This was built next to the grounds of Victory Hall in the 1860s and demolished 100 years later to make way for a housing estate that now stands on its site. **Salacre Lane** led to the house and newer developments are **Salacre Close** and **Salacre Crescent**. Salacres is a derivation of sally carr, named after the marshy land that was in the vicinity.

South of Upton is Woodchurch, which had a population of just 114 in 1841 and many of the current street names there reflect field names from rural times. Examples are **Meadow Crescent**, **Common Field Road** and **Grass Wood Road**. The estate was built on the site of Home Farm, after which **Home Farm Road** is named. This farm covered 285 acres.

In Norman times Woodchurch was ruled by barons from Nantwich, hence **Nantwich Close**. Nearby is **Troutbeck Close**, which is named after Sir John Troutbeck who was Lord of the Manors of Barnston, Oxton and Raby in the 15th century. In 1459 he was killed fighting in the Wars of the Roses at the Battle of Blore Heath. His son William died in 1510 and as he had no direct descendants, the lands passed to the Earls of Shrewsbury by marriage. Another street named after local gentry is **Domville Drive**. This remembers the Domvilles, who lived in Brimstage.

Church Lane leads to the Church of the Holy Cross, which dates from Norman times. Yew trees line the approach to the church and this is reflected nearby with **Yew Tree Close**. Adjoining this is **Archers**

Way, which is so named as yew trees were a source of wood for the bows of archers in medieval times. Someone who used a bow and arrow to good effect was the outlaw Robin Hood, who robbed from the rich to feed the poor in Sherwood Forest, near Nottingham. However, he is not the reason why there is a **Robin Way** situated here. The Robin family were rectors of the church for three generations from 1861 to 1940.

The population of Greasby grew from 290 in 1901 to 4,367 in 1951. In the days when it was just a small village, Greasby's water supply used to be drawn from wells that were situated off Frankby Road near **Pump Lane**, **Old Pump Lane** and **Well Lane**. A pump on Pump Lane fell into disuse after World War 1 but was restored after a campaign in the 1980s.

Shaw Lane remembers local landowner John Ralph Shaw, who built Arrowe Hall between 1835 ad 1844. In 1862 he placed the iron cross in Mill Lane in Greasby, which replaced an earlier stone cross.

In contrast to Greasby, Frankby did not enjoy a population explosion in the first half of the 20th century. Whereas Greasby's increased ten fold, Frankby did not even double in size. One of the few roads here is **Hill Bark Road**, which is named after a hotel and conference centre called Hill Bark House that was first built on a completely different site. The Elizabethan mansion was erected in Bidston Hill in 1891 by soap manufacturer Robert Hudson and named Bidston Court. Between 1929 and 1931 ship owner Ernest Bland Royden dismantled it and moved it to the current location. He named it Hill Bark after an earlier house called Hill Bark that had belonged to his wife's family.

WALLASEY

There could be considerable debate as to what encompasses Wallasey today, as the name of the old village has now been used to describe the surrounding townships of Liscard and Poulton cum Seacombe[1]. Wallasey Town Hall is situated in Seacombe despite Wallasey Village being a mile away and Wallasey's main shopping precinct is actually in Liscard. The coastal resort of New Brighton was never a township in its own right but has always retained a separate identity. For the purpose of this section, I have generally broken the area up into the old township boundaries, but readers may consider some streets to be in another area to where I have described them as being.

In Victorian times Wallasey Village, the oldest inhabited part of modern day Wallasey, was largely agricultural and consisted of just one main street. The name has Saxon origins and refers to being an island. This is because it is surrounded by a ridge on one side and marshes on the other. **Breck Road** is named after this ridge, which, stretches from Poulton to the sea. The term 'breck' means natural heathland or scrub and local streets such as **Breckside Avenue** and **Hillside Road** are named in relation to it.

The high local ground is reflected by **Pennine Road**, named after the Pennine mountain range. **Braemore Road** and **Cromarty Road** are named after places in the Scottish Highlands. Near to these roads is **Millthwaite Road**, which takes its name from a house that stood here on the site of an earlier stone mill that had been built in 1765. A cotton broker named George Peers lived there at the end of the 19th century.

Wallasey's Church of St Hilary is one of less than ten to be named as such in England. A church has stood on this site for over 1,000 years, although the current building dates from 1859 after an earlier structure

---

[1] Wallasey, Liscard and Poulton cum Seacombe were amalgamated in 1910 to form the Borough of Wallasey.

was destroyed by fire in 1857. **St Hilary Brow** and **St Hilary Drive** take their names from the church, although the former was once known as Carren Hill, after a local family. St Nicholas Church in Groveland Road was erected by Frederick Harrison and Sir Heath Harrison in memory of their mother. It has given its name to **St Nicholas Road**, which is in the parish. The Harrison family owned a house that has given its name to a street off Broadway called **The Laund**, the name of which derives from being on a strip of land. In 1901 the family were honoured when **Harrison Drive** was opened, after they had donated the adjoining Harrison Park to the town five years earlier.

Off Wallasey Village, **Stonehouse Road** is named after the Stone House, which was built in 1693 and demolished towards the end of the 19th century. Also here is **Buxton Lane**, named after Buxton House. **Newland Drive** remembers a house called Newlands that used to stand here, while **Mosslands Drive** is named after a house called Mosslands. This was once the home of W Chambers, in whose memory the chiming clock at the Church of St Hilary was placed. **Rolleston Drive** takes its name from a house that was the home of Dr John Oldershaw, who was Mayor of Wallasey in 1911. He had named it after the Leicestershire village from where his wife came.

Clare Mount School was set up by Reverend William Greene and stood opposite Sandy Lane on **Claremount Road** (previously Top Lane). He named it after Clare College, Cambridge, which he attended. **Clare Crescent** and **Clare Way** have also taken their names from this school and developers have continued the theme with a number of local roads being named after famous public schools. **Harrow Road** and **Rugby Road** are named after schools that were founded in the 16th century. Harrow provided the education for two Prime Ministers[2] and Rugby was the inspiration for Thomas Hughes's novel *Tom Brown's School Days*.

Scotland's oldest independent school, situated in Edinburgh, is remembered by **Loretto Road**. Britain's oldest public school is the 14th century Winchester School, after which **Winchester Road**

[2] Sir Robert Peel and Sir Winston Churchill

is named. **Sherborne Road** is named after Sherborne Preparatory School in Dorset, which acts as a feeder to many of England's leading public schools. Other streets named after schools are **Radley Road**, **Sedbergh Road**, **Shrewsbury Road** and **Uppingham Road**. Near to these streets is **School Lane**, although it is not named in relation to Clare Mount. It used to lead to a school for girls and infants that closed in 1907. This road was previously known as Nelson's Gutter, after a George Nelson who lived in a cottage there.

Running alongside Wallasey Golf Course is **Bayswater Road**. An article in the Wallasey News in 1932 suggested that this name came from the fact that it was near to the water of Liverpool Bay. In the same article, the author suggested that **Barmouth Road** was named because the bar and mouth of the River Mersey could be seen from the site. This was a theory that sparked some debate, as there is a Welsh coastal resort named Barmouth and there are other streets in this vicinity that are named after places in Wales. They are **Bangor Road**, **Beaumaris Road** and **Newport Avenue**. Also nearby, North Yorkshire coastal towns have been remembered by **Redcar Road** and **Saltburn Road**.

Before it became a built up area, much of Wallasey was sand hills and this is shown by streets such as **Sandy Lane**, **Sandymount Road** and **Sandcliffe Road**. **Hose Side Road** was named after an old farm that stood near the sand hills. The name derived as a corruption of hoes or hoose, which means sand. Another sand themed street is **Sandiways Road**. This was once known as Jockey Lane, after some racing stables that stood there.

The local shore was once a place where smuggling took place, sometimes after ships had deliberately been forced aground to be looted. Many of the profits and goods were stored at Mother Redcaps in Egremont, which legend states was connected with this area by a labyrinth of local caves. The house, which stood near Lincoln Drive, dated from the late 16th century but after falling in to disrepair was demolished in 1974. Off Sandcliffe Road in Wallasey, **Redcap Close** and **Smugglers Way** are reminders of it.

Prior to 1830 the coastal resort of New Brighton was known as Rock Point. But Liverpool merchant James Atherton saw its potential and bought 170 acres of land with the aim of developing rows of large villas, each one offering a sea view. He named the town New Brighton after the fashionable resort of Brighton that had been developed in Sussex by the Prince Regent.

Although Atherton's dream of a tranquil resort was initially realised, the coming of the railways led to invasions by hordes of holidaymakers from the Lancashire mill towns and ferry day trippers from Liverpool. A cheap terrace of lodgings appeared called the Ham and Egg Parade, named after a cheap dish that was served by the cafes. This was demolished in 1905 and Victoria Gardens constructed, later joined by the Marine Promenade and new sea wall.

Holidaymakers may have disappeared, but New Brighton today remains a popular day trip destination for the people of Wirral and other parts of Merseyside and Cheshire. However, many of the street names retain their links with the era of Joseph Atherton.

Atherton had lived across the Mersey in Everton, which was also an exclusive area with properties that enjoyed river views. By developing an **Atherton Street** in New Brighton, he was continuing a tradition that he had begun in Everton and continued to do so with the development of **Albion Street** and **Albion Place**. Atherton had built an Albion Street in Everton and the name is in relation to the old romantic name for England. Atherton's son-in-law and business partner was William Rowson, after whom **Rowson Street** was named. Both men are buried in the Church of St. Hilary in Wallasey Village. Two examples of streets that are named after houses Atherton built are **Dalmorton Road** and **Sudworth Road**.

The first church to be consecrated was St James Church in 1856, which has given its name to **St James Road**. The first vicar was Richard

Drake Fowell, after whom **Fowell Road** is named.

When New Brighton was being developed the Napoleonic Wars, fought from 1799 to 1815 were still fresh in the mind. This was reflected in some of the street names around the resort, with **Waterloo Road** being named after the Battle of Waterloo. The victorious Arthur Wellesley, Duke of Wellington is remembered by **Wellington Road**. But perhaps the most interesting Napoleonic connected street is **Montpellier Crescent**. This is named after a house, so called because during the hostilities many British families were interred at Montpellier in southern France.

Virtually the whole of New Brighton's development took place when Queen Victoria was on the throne from 1837 to 1901. She is commemorated in the resort by **Victoria Road** and **Victoria Parade**, while her husband is remembered by **Albert Street**. When Albert died in 1861 at the age of just 42, Victoria withdrew from public life for a considerable time and many of her public duties were carried out by her eldest son, Albert Edward. His wife Alexandra has given her name to **Alexandra Road**.

Off Victoria Road, some streets have been named after royal residences. **Balmoral Road** is named after Balmoral Castle in Aberdeenshire, which was built in 1854 on land acquired by Prince Albert and is still used as a royal residence today. A much older residence remembered was Windsor Castle in Berkshire, which has been the site of a royal residence since the 11th century and is commemorated by **Windsor Street**. **Richmond Street** was named after Richmond Palace, which was used by Elizabeth I but is now derelict. Another royal residence has been remembered off Albion Street by **Sandringham Drive**. This was named after Sandringham House in Norfolk, where George VI was born in 1895 and George V died in 1935.

William Lamb, 2nd Viscount Melbourne was Prime Minister in 1834 and from 1835 to 1841. He was a great influence on the young Queen Victoria and introduced her to many ways of statesmanship. He is remembered in the resort by **Melbourne Street**. Melbourne also gave his name to one of Australia's major cities and next to Melbourne Street the Australian city of Brisbane has been commemorated by **Brisbane Avenue**. This city in Queensland was named after Sir Thomas Makdougall Brisbane, who was governor of New South Wales in the early 1820s. He began to utilise the convict inhabitants to develop a colony by clearing the land and encouraging exploration. These two streets are near to **North Drive**, which was named after Frederick North, who owned land in the area and died in 1910.

One of the attractions of the resort was New Brighton Tower, on which construction commenced in 1897. It was 562 feet high and its summit was 621 feet above sea level due to its base, which housed a theatre and ballroom. Taller than Blackpool Tower, it cost 6d to go up in the lift but its fame was short lived. During World War 1 audiences at its attractions dropped and it became unsafe, with no money being available for repairs. It was demolished between 1919 and 1921 although the ballroom and theatre stayed until they were destroyed by fire in 1969.

A housing estate is now situated near where the tower once stood and contains a road called **New Tower Court**. Also present on this estate is **Rakersfield Road** and **Rakersfield Court**, which are named after New Brighton FC, who were known as the Rakers. They played in a sports stadium next to the tower and were members of the Football League on two occasions, from 1898 to 1901 and from 1923 to 1951. All these roads lie off **Molyneux Drive**, which remembers the family who lived on the land before the tower was built. Nearby is **Seymour Street**, named after Lord Seymour.

In 1931 work began on **King's Parade**, which was named after George V. This wide waterfront road was part of a wider plan that was intended to incorporate top quality hotels, but the outbreak of World War 2 put a stop to this. However many felt that the money would have been better spent securing a Wallasey entrance and exit for the new tunnel that was being built under the Mersey between Liverpool and Birkenhead.

The old township of Liscard became a popular residential area after the introduction of ferry services to Liverpool from Seacombe and Egremont in the 1860s. By the end of the 19th century it was well built up, consisting of both large houses for the wealthy and terraced properties.

One of the oldest roads in Liscard is **Rake Lane**, which literally means Lane Lane, as rake is an old word for lane. The old town field of Liscard was situated off this and was served by Townfield Lane. This is now **Urmson Road**, named after an old Liscard family, but the original name still lives on somewhat with **Townfield Way**. An old mill stood near Eric Road and this has given its name to **Mill Lane**.

A major landowner was John Penkett, who became Lord of the Manor around 1800. He was a Liverpool merchant who lived in the Manor House, which was situated on the coast at Egremont. **Penkett Road** commemorates Penkett, while **Manor Road** and **Manor Lane** lead to the site of the house, which was demolished in 1937 after ending its days as an infirmary. When Penkett died his lands were inherited by his daughter Mary, who married John Maddock. She is commemorated by **Maddock Road**. The Manor House was known as Seabank until 1841, which explains the name **Seabank Road** that was cut through the estate. Another local landowner was William Meddowcroft, after whom **Meddowcroft Road** was named.

Liscard Hall was built by Sir John Tobin in 1830. Following the death of his son-in-law Harold Littledale in 1889 it was purchased by the Wallasey Local Board and opened up to the public in 1891. The park has given its name to **Central Park Avenue**, as well as **Parkside** and **Park Street**. In addition, **Serpentine Road** takes its name from the Serpentine, a lake in Hyde Park, London. Another house now in public hands is Earlston, after which **Earlston Road** is named.

Oarside House, after which **Oarside Drive** is named, was part of a dairy farm that was one of the first in the country to bottle milk. This was delivered locally in a fleet of horse drawn milk floats. The road stands off **Mount Pleasant Road**, named after a house that stood where Weatherhead High School now stands. **Pleasant Road** is also named after this house. **Mount Road** takes its name from a house called The Mount, which was a private residence and a school before it was demolished in 1938.

One of the more unusually named houses was Zig Zag Hall, which was named after a twisting lane now known as **Zig Zag Road**. Two owners of the hall are commemorated by **Sheen Road** and **Steel Road**. Mr Sheen bought the hall in 1881 when it was a large farmhouse, going on to extensively redesign and alter it. In 1889 he sold it to Richard Steel, who lived there till he died in 1910. Near to Zig Zag Hall was a house called Withensfield House, which stood on the site of the **Withensfield** cul-de-sac. It was demolished in 1930 after being a YMCA holiday home and **Withens Lane** is named after a field from which the house was named. Also in this vicinity is **Bridgecroft Road**, which also takes its name from a field.

In the 1830s Liverpool brush merchant John Astley Marsden moved to Liscard and built a house that he called Liscard Castle, because of its castle like design. It is no longer in existence but has been remembered by **Castle Road** and **Turret Road**, which have been built near where it stood. Marsdens Lane led to it but around 1850 this was renamed **Seaview Road**, which was another name for the house as it had a sea view. There is also a **Seaview Avenue**, which is adjacent to **Fairview Avenue**. This is named after a house that was lived in by surgical boot maker Minnie Fosbroke in the early 20th century. Completing a trio of 'view' streets here is **Longview Avenue**, which remembers a house that had a large garden.

Mary Ann Maddock, Lady of the Manor, gave the land on which St Mary's Church was built in 1876 and this has given its name to **St Mary's Avenue** and **St Mary's Street**. Also in Liscard, **St Albans Road** is named after St Albans, a Catholic church in Mill Lane. A long gone church is an Anglo Saxon one that was said to stand near **Kirkway**, kirk being an ancient word for church.

Off Liscard Crescent, two residents who contributed greatly to the rise of Wallasey have given their names to **Monk Road** and **Newell Road**. These remember Thomas Monk and his son-in-law, who built the Great Float Docks and Seacombe ferry approaches.

There are a number of streets in Liscard named in relation to the Boer War and these can be found off Zig Zag Road in an area that was once known as 'Little Africa'. They were developed after Lord Strathcona, who is commemorated by **Strathcona Road**, visited Wallasey in 1902. His Canadian regiment, Strathcona's Horse, was a mounted division that was raised specifically for the Boer War but is still in existence today, having served in Bosnia and Afghanistan.

When the Boer War began British troops first mobilised at the port of Durban, after which **Durban Road** is named. **Carrington Road** takes its name from Lieutenant General Sir Frederick Carrington, who commanded troops from Rhodesia. **Glencoe Road** is named after Glencoe in Natal, which was immortalised in a poem by William McGonagall. This was after British forces drove some Boers off Smiths Hill in the Battle of Glencoe in October 1899. The Boer siege of Kimberley was ended in February 1900 by Commander John French, an event commemorated by **Kimberley Road**. Britain used the full weight of the Empire to defeat the Boers, with troops from Australia and Canada fighting in South Africa. This is honoured by **Imperial Road**.

Any ship entering the port of Liverpool had to put its gunpowder into storage for safekeeping. For safety reasons, a remote location was needed and Liscard was chosen in the 1750s. Known as either the Liscard Battery or Magazines, the stores have given rise to the names of **Magazine Avenue**, **Magazine Lane** and **Magazine Brow**. In the 1850s the population of the area was increasing and the stores were moved to three offshore hulks down the river at Bromborough. Near to the Magazines was Vale Park, which was owned by the Holland family, who are commemorated by **Holland Road**.

Moving on to a literary theme, two of Benjamin Disraeli's novels are commemorated in Liscard. **Coningsby Drive** is named after *Coningsby*, published in 1844, while **Tancred Road** takes its name from his 1847 novel *Tancred*. Also in this area is **Burns Avenue**, named after Scottish poet and writer of folk songs Robert Burns. Nearby, by Central Park, **Pendennis Road** commemorates William Makepeace Thackeray's 1848 publication *Pendennis*.

There are some politicians remembered off Liscard Road. **Alverstone Road** is named after Lord Alverstone, who was Lord Chief Justice between 1900 and 1913, while Lord Clarendon, Foreign Secretary in the 1850s gives his name to **Clarendon Road**. **Rosebery Grove** is named after another Foreign Secretary, Philip Archibald Primrose, Earl of Rosebery. He held the position from 1892 to 1894 then succeeded Gladstone as Prime Minister and was in office for fifteen months.

In the 19th century John Askew bought some land around the boundary between Seacombe and Liscard. The house he built was named Egremont after his Cumbrian birthplace. He then developed a pier from which ferries sailed to Liverpool and this became known as the Egremont Ferry, as it was neither nearer to nor further from the other districts. The pier was scrapped in 1946 after twice being damaged by vessels, leading to the cessation of ferry services. But Askew's name lives on locally thanks to **Askew Close**. This is off **Tobin Street**, named after Sir John Tobin who used to take the ferry to his offices in Liverpool. Another person who owned some land here was Ellen King, after whom **King Street** was named. **Marsden Close** remembers John Marsden, who was mentioned earlier as having built Liscard Castle.

Tobin was buried in St Johns churchyard. He had paid for the construction of this church in 1832, building it to a Grecian design. It had the longest unsupported roof span in Cheshire and was able to seat up to 2,000 people and has given its name to **Church Close**, **Church Street**, **Churchmeadow Close** and **St John's Road**.

Streets in Egremont named in relation to the Napoleonic Wars include **Trafalgar Avenue** and **Trafalgar Road**, as well as **Nelson Street**. Wellington's London home of Apsley House is remembered by **Apsley Avenue**. Another street in Egremont is **Fort Street**, named after Fort Perch Rock, situated on a sandstone rock outcrop off New Brighton beach. The fort was first proposed as a permanent defence for Liverpool early on in the Napoleonic Wars, but after the Battle of Trafalgar fears of a French invasion eased. Plans were reactivated in the 1820s and the fort opened in 1830. However it only ever fired one shot in anger, across the bow of a Norwegian fishing vessel in World War 1 when it failed to identify itself.

Off Seabank Road in Egremont, two royal residences from the Victorian period have streets named after them. Marlborough House had been built in the early 18th century and was the residence of Edward VII before he became King at the age of 59 in 1901. It has given its name to **Marlborough Road** and is currently in use as offices for the Commonwealth Secretariat. **Osborne Avenue** was named after Osborne House on the Isle of Wight, which was built as a holiday home between 1845 and 1851. Victoria died there in 1901 and the Italianate mansion is now open as a tourist attraction to provide an insight into her life.

In 1882 The Liverpool Home for Ancient Mariners was built in Egremont. This was following a donation from Liverpool ship owner William Cluff after his daughter Rosa Webster died. The home is now demolished but the streets that have replaced it, which include **Webster Avenue**, have a maritime theme. **Ismay Avenue** is named after Thomas Ismay, founder of the White Star Line, one of the most prominent Transatlantic liner services that sailed out of Liverpool. One of their fiercest competitors was Cunard, after which **Cunard Avenue** is named. Also present is **Royden Avenue**, which was named after Thomas Royden. He owned a ship building yard in Liverpool that was later closed down by his son, Thomas Bland Royden, who then founded the Indra Line.

Local politicians remembered in Egremont are Joseph Walmsley of the Wallasey U.D.C.[3] and Albert T Wright of Cheshire County Council. **Walmsley Street** and **Wright Street** are named after them. Round the corner from Walmsley Street is **Churchill Grove**. This was named after Lord Randolph Churchill, who was Chancellor of the Exchequer in the 1880s.

During the second half of the 19th century Seacombe changed beyond recognition. This was due to the continuing growth of ferry services to Liverpool and the development of industry around Wallasey Pool. As a consequence, green and leafy lanes gave way to row upon row of terraced housing.

The main street in 1850 had been Victoria Road. But following the amalgamation of the three townships in 1910 this was changed to **Borough Road** at the request of the fire brigade. This was to prevent confusion with Victoria Road in New Brighton. **Oakdale Road** and **Oakdale Avenue** remember Oakdale Farm, which remembers a time when the area was a small valley with oak trees and a stream.

Near to Seacombe Promenade, **Demesne Street** is named in relation to an area of land that only the lords of the manor could use. In 1800 it was owned by Rear Admiral Smith, who was Lord of the Manor of Poulton. In the early 18th century one of the main landowners in Liscard were the Mainwaring family, who originated from Shropshire. They are remembered in Seacombe by **Mainwaring Road**.

Byerley Street remembers Dr Isaac Byerley, who lived nearby in the late 19th century. D.B. Rappart, who played a part in the development of Wallasey between 1884 and 1914, has been remembered by **Rappart Road**. For many years in the first half of the 19th century, the Seacombe Ferry was leased by Mr T. Parry, who also ran Parry's Seacombe Hotel. He lived at Brougham House, which has given its name to **Brougham Road**. A dower house to Wallasey Hall stood on the site of Harlech Street. This was known as Wheatland House and is remembered by

Wheatland Lane.

A Seacombe church that was a local landmark to sailors was St Paul's. Its tall spire was one of the first things that could be seen when approaching the town from the sea and hence it became known as the 'sailor's church'. The spire is no longer there but the church has given its name to **St Paul's Road**, **St Paul's Avenue**, **Church Road** and **Church Crescent**. The writers of three of the four Gospels of the New Testament have also been named in relation to this church. They are Mark, Matthew and Luke, after whom **Mark Street**, **Matthew Street** and **Luke Street** are named. Although they didn't write any of the Gospels, Saints James and Peter were two important Apostles, being early leaders of the Church in Jerusalem and Rome. They are remembered here by **James Street** and **Peter Street**.

One of the streets in Seacombe named in relation to royalty is **Leopold Street**. This is named after Leopold, Duke of Albany, who was the fourth and youngest son of Queen Victoria. Two of his brother Edward VII's children are commemorated by streets in Seacombe. **Clarence Road** is named after Prince Albert Victor, Duke of Clarence and Avondale, who died in 1892. That meant that his brother George, Duke of York became Heir Apparent and would eventually become King George V in 1910 after the death of his father. **York Road**, which is next to Clarence Street, is named after him.

Near these streets is **Naples Road**, which may have been named because Victoria's husband Albert felt the views over the Rover Solent from Osborne House in the Isle of Wight were similar to the Bay of Naples. Also in Seacombe, **Albemarle Road** commemorates Lord Albemarle, who was Master of the Horse in 1837. This job entailed heading the Royal Mews, where the queen's horses were kept.

Literary streets in Seacombe include **Shakespeare Street** and **Abbotsford Street**. The latter is named after Abbotsford House, situated in the Scottish Borders and the home of novelist Sir Walter Scott. He lived there from 1820 until his death in 1832.

West of Seacombe, **Poulton Road** leads to Poulton, which means the 'town by the pool'. At the end of this, near its junction with Mill Lane is **Poulton Hall Road**. This is named after Poulton Hall, which was built in 1800 and demolished in 1933 to make way for the houses that now stand there. At the beginning of the 20th century it was the home of Alfred Hopps, an oil merchant. Leading from here to the docks is **Limekiln Lane**, which derives from some limekilns that stood near the edge of Wallasey Pool at the beginning of the 19th century.

An old family who lived in this area were the Sherlocks, who are remembered by **Sherlock Lane**. Captain Sherlock was the last captain of a Liverpool to Seacombe ferry that used sails before the advent of steam powered crossings in the 1820s.

On the opposite side of Poulton Road is **Balfour Road**. This was named after Arthur James Balfour, who was Prime Minister from 1902 to 1905. Next to this is **Chamberlain Street**, which takes its name from Joseph Chamberlain, who had been President of the Board of Trade in 1880 and Colonial Secretary twenty years later during the Boer War. A former queen is remembered by **Adelaide Street**. This was named after Adelaide of Saxe-Meiningen, who was the wife of William IV. He reigned from 1830 to 1837 but the two children she bore him died in infancy meaning that his niece, 18 year old Victoria, became Queen upon his death.

LEASOWE AND MORETON

The name Leasowe derives from the Anglo Saxon Leasowes, meaning 'meadow pastures'. Prior to the 1920s much of Leasowe was sand dunes and marshes and this is reflected in the present names of **The Sandhills** and **Marshfield Court**. At one time the only land entrance to the parish was **Green Lane**, which was literally a strip of green land where no farming took place.

Leasowe Castle was built by Ferdinando, 5th Earl of Derby in 1593, a year before he became Lord of the Manor of Wallasey. After many additions over the years it is now in use as a hotel and has given its name to **Castle Close**, **Castleford Rise**, **Castlegrange Close**, **Castleheath Close**, **Castleway North** and **Castleway South**. Just south of here, the River Birket flows towards Birkenhead and has given its name to **Birket Avenue**, **Birket Close** and **Birket Square**.

The first racecourse in Britain may well have been at Leasowe. Situated on flat land behind the sand dunes that was ideal for racing, races were run from early in the 17th Century for nearly 200 years. The practice stopped in the 1790s and the land became used for market gardening, but some streets today are named after racecourses from around the country.

Epsom Drive and **Epsom Road** are named after Surrey's Epsom Racecourse. Britain's most famous flat race, The Derby, has been run here since 1780. **Cheltenham Crescent** takes its name from

Cheltenham Racecourse, where the Cheltenham National Hunt Festival is held. Staying in southern England, **Newbury Way** and **Goodwood Drive** are named after racecourses in Berkshire and Sussex. A course nearer to home that is commemorated is Aintree, which gives its name to **Aintree Close**. The world's most famous steeplechase, run over jumps, takes place there every April.

Horse Racing isn't the only sport commemorated in Leasowe. New Brighton RUFC play at a ground in Reeds Lane and nearby, the national stadiums of English and Scottish rugby are commemorated by **Murrayfield Drive** and **Twickenham Drive**.

Before World War 1 Leasowe became a popular destination for people on camping holidays. Near to the station, Kingsmead Field was run by Mr J Cole and from the 1930s more permanent structures were erected there, leading to the naming of **Kingsmead Road**. Not far away, Avondale Park was owned by the Osborne family and could accommodate 75 caravans. This has been remembered by **Avondale Road**.

Around the same time as the caravan parks were developing, many farms were being sold for development. Two examples that have streets named after them were situated off Leasowe Road by Our Lady of Lourdes School. Leasoweside Farm was sold in the 1930s by the Sutton family who had been there for 100 years, but its name has lived on in **Leasoweside**. Nearby was Liscard Farm, which was run as a market garden, hence the street name of **Gardenside**.

Reeds Avenue, **Reeds Avenue West** and **Reeds Lane** were named after Reeds farm, which was also worked by the Sutton family. Running between the two avenues is **Farmside**, which is where the farm stood.

Between Leasowe Road and Bidston Golf Course several streets have been named after explorers, possibly because of Leasowe's proximity to the sea. Sir Francis Drake, the first Englishman to circumnavigate the world in 1579 gives his name to **Drake Road**. He later introduced tobacco to England and defeated the Spanish Armada in 1588, but died on another mission to the Caribbean in 1595 when he contracted dysentery. Another Elizabethan explorer to be commemorated is Sir Martin Frobisher, after whom **Frobisher Road** is named. In 1576 he mistakenly thought he had found the North West Passage, a much sought after northern route from the Atlantic to Pacific oceans. However it was simply a bay that is now known as Frobisher Bay, off Baffin Island, which lies between Canada and Greenland.

Frobisher was followed in his quest to find the North West Passage by Henry Hudson, who is remembered by **Hudson Road**. He made four attempts to locate it between 1607 and 1611, before eventually being cast adrift never to be heard of again when his crew mutinied after their ship, Discovery, was frozen in by ice for three months. However he did make a lasting impression across the Atlantic when he explored the Hudson River, which flows through New York. The Discovery was then piloted on a new Atlantic mission by William Baffin in another attempt to find the North West Passage. He sailed to a position of 77 degrees 45 north in 1616. No other man went this far north for 236 years. On that voyage he named Baffin Island and in Leasowe he gives his name to **Baffin Close**.

The search for the North West Passage was still ongoing over 200 years later. **Ross Avenue** is named after Sir James Clark Ross, who accompanied his uncle John Ross on an unsuccessful mission in 1818. He went on to make other Arctic expeditions and discovered the magnetic North Pole in 1831. Another mission was led by Sir John Franklin, who went missing in 1846. Search parties were sent out and it was established that his ship was icebound for nine months before he died in June 1847, with some crew members surviving until the following April. **Franklin Road** is named after him. Antarctic explorer Sir Ernest Henry Shackleton gives his name to **Shackleton Road**. He undertook the first attempt to reach the South Pole in 1909, coming within 111 miles of it.

An explorer who stuck to land was Sir Alexander Mackenzie, who is remembered by **Mackenzie Road**. He was a Scot who emigrated to Canada and became the first man to explore the USA and Canada overland in the late 18th century. A more modern explorer is Louise Arner Boyd, an American who undertook a number of Arctic expeditions prior to World War 2. In 1955, at the age of 68, she became the first woman to fly over the North Pole and has given her name to **Boyd Close**. Finally for explorers, David Livingstone, who is covered in Birkenhead, is honoured by **Livingstone Road**.

Moreton, which is Anglo Saxon for 'lake town' was once known as Moreton-cum-Lingham but the Lingham was eventually dropped. Lingham Farm stands north of the railway line near the disused lighthouse. **Lingham Lane** leads to this and there is also a **Lingham Close**. The name Lingham is Norse and means 'heather island'. For many centuries Moreton remained a small farming community and the main street through the old village was on the site of the current **Pasture Road**.

Moreton's farming past is shown today in street names such as **Berrylands Road**, **Bramble Way**, **Garden Lane** and **Harvest Lane**. A building that had to be demolished to make way for these developments was Felicity Cottage, which stood on the site of **Felicity Grove** for 100 years prior to 1948. **Danger Lane** implies that there may once have been a perilous route in Moreton, but in fact the name derives from dangh, an old word for black shale. In the second half of the 17th century, an Irish peer named Lord Kingston held land in Moreton and Bidston. This is reflected in **Kingston Close**.

In 1841 the turnpike road that is now **Hoylake Road** was created. It was known as Birkenhead Road, Hoylake Road, Main Road or Village Road and the current name was formally settled on when Moreton was incorporated into the district of Wallasey in 1928. Another old road was Back Lane or Chapel Lane, which is now named **Barnton Lane**. **Maryland Lane** was once known as Mary Anne's Lane, after the owner of a cottage there, or as Town Meadow Lane. After absorption into Wallasey, the lane was officially named with one section becoming Maryland Lane and the rest **Town Meadow Lane**.

Another road to be renamed was Cecil Avenue, which became **Griffin Avenue** to avoid confusion with Cecil Road in Wallasey. Canon Griffin was a member of the Borough Council and the Church of the Sacred Heart. The street had originally been named after Robert Gascoyne Cecil, Marquis of Salisbury, who was Prime Minister from 1885 to 1892. However, two streets are still named after Salisbury. Firstly there is **Childwall Avenue**, named after Childwall Hall in Liverpool, which his family owned. The second is **Cranbourne Avenue**, after the title of Viscount Cranbourne that was given to the Marquis's eldest son. Another Prime Minister honoured in Moreton is Winston Churchill, after whom **Winston Grove** is named.

Salisbury and Churchill were both Conservative, but near Lingham Park some socialist politicians have been remembered. **Hardie Avenue** is named after James Keir Hardie, who went down the mines of Lanarkshire when he was twelve but learnt to read and write and went on to found the Labour Party. **Macdonald Road** takes its name from Ramsay Macdonald, who helped Hardie found the Labour Party in 1900 and went on to become their first Prime Minister in January 1924. High unemployment led to the fall of his government within a year but he returned to office in 1929. He remained Prime Minister for six years until 1935, but the last four of these were as head of a coalition government. Macdonald's Chancellor of the Exchequer in 1924 and from 1929 to 1931 was Philip Snowden, who is remembered by **Snowden Road**. Nearby, off Wastdale Drive, is **Glasier Road**. This is named after John Bruce Glasier, a chief leader of the Socialist movement in Scotland in the late 19th century. He became a founder member of the Labour Party, but would never win a seat in the House of Commons.

Millhouse Lane is named after Millhouse Farm, which had taken its name from an old mill that fell down in 1870 when the last miller, Richard Hale, left. The farm remained in operation until the 1950s and was sometimes known as Jordan's Farm, after its owners. Off Millhouse

Lane are **Broster Avenue** and **Broster Close**. These streets are named after a family who for many generations lived in Ivy Cottage, a 300+ year old building on Saughall Massie Road.

Some streets in Moreton have been named after wading birds, due to the fact many visit Wirral's north coast while migrating in spring or autumn. They are **Curlew Way**, **Mallard Way** and **Tern Way**.

Moreton has almost swallowed up Saughall Massie. This name comes from a corner where willows grow and has been reflected in street names there such as **Birchfield** and **The Cedars**.

Near where Saughall Road meets Hoylake Road, The Grange estate was built in the 1930s and named after a large house of the same name that had been demolished to make way for development. This had been built in the late 1800s for the Griffith family who dealt in horse transport. The street names of the new estate have been named after parts of the old estate and they are **The Paddock**, **Coppice Grange** and **Orchard Grange**.

HOYLAKE AND MEOLS

The name Hoylake comes from a sandbank that stretched along the coast to Meols creating a lake like safe haven for ships. Being sheltered, this meant that Hoylake was important as an anchorage for ships on their way to Chester and also as an embarkation point for Ireland. The word 'Hoyle' derives from the word 'hillock', meaning small mound or hill, hence **Hoyle Road**. In addition to this **Lake Road** derives from the lake and next to this is **Strand Road**, which is a word meaning shore. From the early 18th century Hoylake's role declined due to the growth of the port of Liverpool and silting up of the River Dee.

The most famous person to have sailed from Hoylake was King William III in 1690. He embarked for Ireland to confront James II, who was trying to regain the throne from which William had ousted him two years earlier. He had spent the night prior to sailing at Gayton Hall and went on to beat James in the Battle of the Boyne, ensuring that the English monarchy remained Protestant. **The King's Gap** is the route that William took to board his vessel.

Despite going into decline as a port, Hoylake did continue to serve as a safe harbour for ships waiting to enter the Mersey in rough weather. In 1763 Liverpool Corporation built a lighthouse, which was later rebuilt in 1865. It was last used in 1885, but is still in existence today as part of a residence, having been used by the Royal Observer Corp in World War 2. The lighthouse has given rise to the name **Lighthouse Road**.

The local Lord of the Manor in the late 18th century was Sir John Stanley. He built the Royal Hotel in 1792 in what was to become **Stanley Road**. The hotel was developed with bathers in mind and **Beach Road** connected it with the beach. Hoylake developed as a pleasant resort for bathing and boating but didn't become full of cheap lodging and eating houses like New Brighton. **North Parade** was laid out along the seafront in the 1890s.

South of the now demolished Royal Hotel was a rabbit warren on which horse racing began in 1840. In 1869 the Royal Liverpool Golf Club was founded and the two sports co-habited uneasily for seven years before golf took over. The course will be the centre of world attention when it hosts The Open Championship in 2006. **Warren Road** is named in relation to the rabbit warren.

In 1812 the Manor was purchased by Liverpool's Collector of Customs, Timothy Swainson. He built a house called The Dale as a summer residence. It is no longer in existence but has been responsible for the naming of four local streets. They are **Avondale Road**, **Clydesdale Road**, **Dovedale Road** and **Ferndale Road**. In 1833 Swainson's widow financed the construction of Hoylake Trinity Church, after which **Trinity Road** is named. This had to be demolished in 1976 because it was structurally unsound.

Hoylake's population grew significantly after the opening of the railway station in 1866, increasing to 6,352 in 1901 from just 924 forty years earlier. **Station Road** leads to the station.

In addition to William III, two other kings have been commemorated in Hoylake by **Edward Road** (Edward VII) and **George Road** (George V). Edward's father, Albert, husband of Queen Victoria has given his name to **Albert Road**. George V's wife, Queen Mary, gave her name to **Queen's Road**. Prior to World War 1 it was known as Prussia Street but changed due to its Germanic connections. **Sandringham Avenue** is named after the royal residence of Sandringham House.

Where The King's Gap meets Barton Road, two streets have been named after statesmen who looked after British interests abroad. **Cromer Road** remembers Evelyn Baring, 1st Earl Cromer. Except for a three year stint in India, he administered Egypt between 1879 and 1907. **Curzon Road** is named after George Nathaniel Curzon, 1st Marquess Curzon of Kedleston. He was Viceroy of India from 1898 to 1905 and after returning to England served as Foreign Secretary from 1919 to 1924.

One of Scotland's greatest literary figures, Sir Walter Scott (1771-1832) has two streets named after him in Hoylake. Scott trained as a lawyer and combined this with writing poetry, turning down the opportunity to become Poet Laureate in 1813. He then switched to novels and averaged one a year until his death. **Marmion Road** is named after his 1808 Romantic poem *Marmion* and **Waverley Road** after his first novel *Waverley*, published in 1814.

To the east of Hoylake lies Meols, which before the oncoming of the **Birkenhead Road** in 1850 had a population of little more than 100. The development of this road meant that Meols was now connected with the Woodside Hotel and ferry service to Liverpool by omnibus. After spending many years going to church in Hoylake, plans for a place of worship in Meols were finally made in 1901 after the population had reached 800. First a temporary structure was built, which became the church hall when the Church of St John the Baptist was finally consecrated in 1913. This has given its name to **St Johns Close**. For twenty years prior to 1901, services had been held in the school, from which **School Lane** is named.

Although comparatively small in population, Meols is one of the oldest inhabited areas of Wirral. It has been the home to many different settlers for over 2,000 years and these have been remembered in many local street names.

Excavations in the Meols area have uncovered more Roman artefacts than anywhere else on the peninsula. The settlement appears to have been connected with Chester with a road that ran through Willaston and Greasby. These Roman origins are remembered by **Roman Road**, **Centurion Drive** and **Centurion Close**. A centurion was a Roman officer who would be responsible for an army unit of 100 men.

Celtic Road is named after the Celts, who spread across Europe in the 1st Century B.C. They were followed 500 years later by the Saxons, who began to conquer Britain in the 5th Century AD. In Meols they are remembered by **Saxon Road**, while two of their kings also have roads named after them. These are **Egbert Road** and **Ethelbert Road**. Ethelbert was a Saxon king of Kent in the 6th Century, while Egbert was the first Saxon to be recognised as king of all the English kingdoms from 829 till his death in 839.

However, any Saxon and Roman settlements would have been preceded by a 5,000 year old forest that is now submerged off the coast. The tree stumps of this forest could once be seen regularly beneath the sea and wood from it was used for some panelling in Leasowe Castle. But as the sea has encroached further on the land it has only been seen twice since World War 2, in 1947 and 1982. The forest has given its name to **Forest Close**, **Forest Road**, **Edgewood Road**, **The Glade** and **Woodland Avenue**. The earliest inhabitants of Meols may have lived at Dove Point, which once projected well out to sea but is now largely underwater and gives its name to **Dovepoint Road**. The word dove means black and is in relation to the colour of the sea due to the submerged forest.

WEST KIRBY, GRANGE & CALDY

West Kirby was first settled in the Norse period, with the name meaning west of Kirby in Walea, the original name for Wallasey. For many centuries, it was no more than just a small cluster of buildings around the corner of Grange Road and Dee Lane. The latter led down to the River Dee and remains the route that most people take down to the beach, while **Grange Road** led to Grange.

The focal point of the old village was St Bridget's Church, which was first built in Norse times, although the oldest part of the present structure dates from 1150. The church has undergone many changes and the last restoration was in 1870. It has given rise to the names of **St Bridget's Lane**, **Church Road** and **Church Walk**, as well as **Rectory Road**. This is named after the church's rectory that is situated off **Village Road**, historically the main road through West Kirby. **Leigh Road** is named after John Shaw Leigh, who was Lord of the Manor in the early 19th century.

West Kirby's rail link to Liverpool, developed in 1878, allowed commuters to work in the city and live in peaceful surroundings near the sea. This meant that the population rose five fold between 1871 and 1901 and the land south of Grange Road was soon built upon. There is a coastal feel in some of West Kirby's street names such as **Banks Road**, **Sandy Lane** and **Riverside**, although the first two of these were present prior to major development.

The Marine Lake, a major watersports attraction, was first opened in 1899 and used to include an open air swimming pool. Behind this, there once stood a building called the Hydropathic Hotel, which was built in 1890. This offered guests a variety of baths, including Russian, Turkish and salt water. **Hydro Avenue** takes its name from the hotel.

At the south end of the lake a small sandstone building shaped like a castle tower is situated in the grounds of a modern residence. Known as Tells Tower, it was built in 1871 by John Cumming MacDona, who was a local barrister and MP for Rotherhithe in London. MacDona bred St Bernard dogs and built the tower in honour of his champion dog Tell, who died aged seven. He lived at Hilbre House and is remembered by **MacDona Drive**.

The Presbyterian Church on Meols Drive was opened in 1890. It is on the site of an earlier cast iron church, which had been built over a duck pond. The road leading to it had been known as Duck Alley, but is now called **Bridge Road**.

Holm Hill and **Wetstone Lane** are named after Wetstone House, that later became Holm Hill. In the early 20th century it was the home of James Bibby, an oil cake manufacturer. **The Kirklands** takes its name from a house of the same name that stood off Village Road. **Abbey Road**, **Monks Way** and **Priory Road** are named after Abbey Manor, which was sited at the junction of Abbey Road and Grange Road.
Other streets in West Kirby that have been named after large houses include **Heatherdene Road**, **Hillview Avenue** and **Homestead Mews**.

Like many other parts of Wirral, West Kirby has streets named after Queen Victoria and her husband Prince Albert. They are **Victoria Drive**, **Victoria Road** and **Albert Road**. Their son Edward VII's wife Alexandra of Denmark is commemorated by **Alexandra Road**. Edward's successor was George V, who was bestowed the title Duke of York in 1892, eighteen years before he would become king. **York Avenue** commemorates this.

Streets with a literary theme include **Wordsworth Walk**, named after William Wordsworth. Another street here named after a poet is **Shelley Way**. This commemorates Percy Bysshe Shelley (1792-1822), who wrote in a Romantic style like Wordsworth. Most of his work was produced whilst touring in Italy during the last four years of his life, where he tragically drowned after sailing from Livorno.

East of West Kirby is Grange, which remained tranquil during West Kirby's rapid development in the latter part of the 19th century. However in the 20th century there has been a great deal of development.

On Grange Hill stands a sandstone column known as the Beacon, after which **Column Road** is named. This was built in 1841 by the Trustees of Liverpool Docks, as a landmark for shipping. It replaced a mill that had blown down two years earlier. In Grange, the beacon has also given its name to **Beacon Drive**.

Grammar School Lane leads to Calday Grange Grammar School. This is Wirral's oldest school, having been founded as the Grange Free Grammar School in 1636 by William Glegg. In the mid 19th century it suffered a period of decline but the sale of lands generated new funds for investment. This led to the construction of the current building in 1886. The Glegg family had been local Lords of the Manor until 1785 and are remembered by **Gleggside**.

Two streets off Ennisdale Drive are named after heroes of World War 2. **Douglas Road** remembers William Sholto Douglas, who commanded air operations in the Battle of Britain and American led invasion of France. **Slessor Avenue** is named after Sir John Cotesworth Slessor, an RAF marshal who oversaw anti-submarine manoeuvres in the Battle of the Atlantic.

To the north east of Grange is China Farm, after which **China Farm Lane** is named. This farm is so called due to a large china plate that is set into the front wall of the farmhouse.

At the beginning of the 20th century Caldy was mainly woodland, except for the Manor House, which had been built by Manchester businessman Richard Barton in 1832. He had built it to reside in himself and it is now a complex of retirement homes.

One of the first developments in Caldy was **Kings Drive**, which was developed during the reign of Edward VII (1901-1910). The Barton family line has now died out but their name lives on with **Barton Hey Drive**. The word hey derives from an enclosed piece of land.

A small group of streets in Caldy are named after naval commanders from both world wars. **Jellicoe Close** is named after John Rushworth Jellicoe, who was Commander in Chief of the Grand Fleet and won the Battle of Jutland in May 1916, World War 1's most decisive naval battle. This victory gave Britain and its Allies control of the North Sea and hence blockaded the German coast. In November 1916, Jellicoe moved on to submarine operations and was succeeded as Commander of the Grand Fleet by Sir David Beatty, who had been his deputy at Jutland. After the war he went on to become first Lord of the Admiralty and is remembered by **Beatty Close**.

Andrew Browne Cunningham served in the Boer War and commanded a vessel in World War 1, but his most outstanding achievements came in World War 2. As Commander in Chief of the Allied forces in the Mediterranean, he received the surrender of the Italians at Malta and returned to become Admiral of the fleet. After the war he was made a viscount and he is commemorated by **Cunningham Close**.

HESWALL & GAYTON

Heswall and the adjoining township of Gayton grew at a rapid pace in the second half of the 18th century, having been in existence for several hundred years.

The Church of St Peter gives its name to **St Peters Close**. The tower of the church is over 500 years old but the main building was only built in 1879 after the previous structure was destroyed in a thunderstorm. **Farr Hall Road** and **Farr Hall Drive** remember a medieval manor house to the north of the church known as the further hall or farr hall to distinguish it from Gayton Hall, which was built in 1663.

School Hill takes its name from a school that was once situated in Richmond Hall, which is now a community building. This was built in 1872 and enlarged several times until a replacement was built in 1961.

Like many other places in Wirral Heswall commemorates Queen Victoria, this time with **Victoria Avenue**. Also present here is **Stathearn Road**. This is named after her third son, Price Arthur, Duke of Connaught and Strathearn.

The high elevation of Heswall is shown by street names such as **The Mount**, **Brow Lane** and **Dee View Road**. Heswall has never had a castle, but still has a street named **Castle Drive**. This was named after a castellated building called Tytherington's Folly, which was also known as Heswall Castle. It was built in 1870 and by 1900 was a female orphan asylum. It was demolished in 1935.

Roscote Close and **The Roscote** remember Roscote, the country home of shipping magnate Thomas Brocklebank. It was built in the 1860s and demolished 100 years later. **Downham Drive**, **Downham Road North** and **Downham Road South** take their names from a local family. A farm named Hillside has given its name to **Hillside Road**.

Station Road lies some distance from Heswall's railway station. The reason for this is because it remembers another station of some years ago, that was situated on the Hooton to West Kirby line. This line was first opened in 1866 as far as Parkgate then extended to Heswall and West Kirby twenty years later. It was closed to passengers in 1956 and continued as a freight line until 1962. In 1969 it was purchased by Cheshire County Council and converted into the Wirral Way, an attractive countryside walk. However the line around Heswall station was sold off for development in 1966, and was the only part of the line built upon. Next to the station that is still in use and connects Heswall with Bidston and Wrexham is **Pullman Close**, named after a type of railway car.

Adjoining Heswall to the north west is the hamlet of Oldfield, which is reached by **Oldfield Road**. It was once a separate manor and the 16th century Oldfield Hall is now a farmhouse, with **Oldfield Farm Lane** leading to it. There is also an **Oldfield Drive**, **Oldfield Close** and **Oldfield Way**.

Mill Lane, **Gayton Mill Close** and **Old Mill Close** take their names from an old sandstone flour mill whose tower still stands in the housing development. This was built in 1735 on a sandstone ridge, which has been reflected in **The Ridgeway**. Just south of here there was once a reservoir, hence **Well Lane**. **Baskervyle Road** remembers a house of the same name, which was named after the Baskervyles, who became Lords of the Manor in 1758.

Cottage Lane, **Cottage Drive East** and **Cottage Drive West** lead to the old ferry cottage. This is a reminder of days gone by when people would converge on Gayton from all over the Wirral and parts of Wales for the Wakes. Nearby are **Riverbank Road**, **Riverbank Close** and **Seabank Road**. However these streets are something of a misnomer, as the Dee is largely out of sight due to the endless marshes. Near here is **Wittering Lane**, which is named after the owner of a local field.

To the east of Heswall and Gayton is the small village of Thornton Hough. This name came about when the daughter of landowner Roger de Thornton married Richard de Hogh in the 14th century. The first church to be built in the village was All Saints in 1862, after which **Church Road** is named. This was paid for by Joseph Hirst, a textile manufacturer from Huddersfield who owned a lot of land in the village at the time.

However most of the village was developed at the end of the 19th century by Viscount Leverhulme, who also founded Port Sunlight. He purchased Thornton Manor in 1888 and made it the principle home for his family. Leverhulme built the Norman style St. Georges Church, after which **Saint George's Way** is named, as well as developing a smithy that is still in operation today. **Smithy Hill** is named after this. Thornton Manor remained in the hands of the family until the death of the third and last Lord Leverhulme in 2000, aged 85. It is connected to the village by **Manor Road**.

North of Heswall is Pensby. In 1921 its population was just 197 but this had risen to 3,000 by 1951. The main road through the village, **Pensby Road**, was once known as Pensby Lane. At the beginning of the century the general store was run by W J Anderson and he is remembered by **Anderson Close**. One local builder who developed Pensby was John 'Cornelius' Devaney. He named **Cornelius Drive** after himself and **Brian Avenue** after his son.

There are some streets named after sailors between the western ends of Fishers Lane and Kylemore Drive. **Nelson Drive** is named after

63

naval hero Admiral Lord Nelson and off this is **Grenville Drive**. This remembers Sir Richard Grenville, who headed an expedition in 1585 to set up a colony at Roanoke Island off North Carolina. Six years later he was killed by the Spanish in an expedition to the Azores. Running in an 'L' shape between these two roads is **Columbus Drive**, which is named after Christopher Columbus, the discoverer of North America.

Also in this vicinity are roads named in relation to World War 2. **Portal Road** remembers Charles Frederick Algernon Portal, who was Chief Marshal of the RAF, leading Bomber Command. Off this are **Portal Mews** and **Gibson Close**, which is named after Guy Penrose Gibson. He was a squadron commander who was awarded the Victoria Cross in 1943 for deliberately drawing enemy fire away from his colleagues during a mission over the Mohne Dam in North Rhine-Westphalia. He was killed the following year when his plane crashed for an unknown reason over Holland. Harold Rupert Leofric George Alexander gives his name to **Alexander Drive**. He led the evacuation of British troops from Dunkirk in 1942 before moving to North Africa to lead the drive on Tunis and invasion of Sicily. He was later Defence Minister from 1952 to 1954.

Possibly the site of a Roman settlement, Irby remained largely unspoilt until the 20th century. **Mill Hill Road** is named after an old peg mill that stood near the corner of Arrowe Brook Lane and was demolished in 1898. When it was taken down, there was nearly tragedy when three workmen set about dismantling it wrongly. After a large crack appeared they got out of the way and it fell down just seconds later on the very spot where they had been standing.

Running between Irby and Arrowe Park is **Limbo Lane**. This may imply that it is a lane where walkers don't know where they are, but it is actually a corruption of the old Limbers Lane. This was named after two fields, Big Limbers and Little Limbers.

Six residents of Irby perished in World War 1. One of these, Frank Lester was awarded the Victoria Cross for his bravery when he was killed in action at Neuvilly in northern France just one month before the war ended. He is commemorated by **Lester Drive**.

Thurstaston has stayed largely untouched by the development of surrounding areas. **Church Lane** is named after St Bartholomew's Church, which was consecrated in 1886. This replaced a plain stone edifice, built in 1824 and the tower of which still stands in the churchyard. This building was on the site of an even earlier church that had dated from the 12th century. **School Lane** was named after the Dawpool School, which moved here in 1906. It had initially been situated in Station Road, having been founded in 1858 by Joseph Hegan who owned the local Estate.

Station Road, which leads to the Dee Estuary, is named as it led to a station that used to stand on the West Kirby-Hooton line. Thomas Ismay, owner of the White Star Line, who lived at the Dawpool mansion, ensured that this did not run through the village. Determined to maintain tranquillity of village life, he also had the Chester highway (Telegraph Road) re-routed away from the village and closed the old village inn, the Dog and Partridge.

Thingwall was mentioned in the Domesday Book, but by 1801 the population was still only 52. However at the beginning of the 20th century there was much more development, with the population trebling between 1911 and 1931 to over 600.

Sparks Lane was an unnamed path when a farm was built there in the 1850s. When Jack Sparks took over in the 1880s it took his name. Running off this is **Quarry Lane**, which led to the now filled in Thingwall Quarry. **Mill Road** is named after a windmill that was demolished at the end of the 19th century after a sail blew off.

Aberdeen Street 12
Abbey Road 58
Abbots Drive 21
Abbotsford Street 45
Adelaide Road 12
Adelaide Street 46
Ainsdale Close 27
Aintree Close 47
Alabama Way 20
Albany Road 13
Albemarle Road 45
Albert Road (Birkenhead) 13
Albert Road (Hoylake) 54
Albert Road (West Kirby) 58
Albert Street 37
Albion Place 36
Albion Street 36
Alexander Drive 64
Alexandra Drive 13
Alexandra Road (New Brighton) 37
Alexandra Road (West Kirby) 58
Alma Street 10
Alton Road 16
Alverstone Road 42
Alwen Street 13
Anderson Close 63
Apsley Avenue 42
Apsley Grove 22
Archers Way 31
Ark Royal Way 19
Arthur Street 13
Askew Close 42
Asquith Avenue 12
Atherton Street 36
Avondale Road (Hoylake) 54
Avondale Road (Leasowe) 48
Baffin Close 49
Balfour Road 46

Balls Road 16
Balls Road East 16
Balmoral Road 37
Bangor Road 35
Banks Road 57
Barmouth Road 35
Barnton Lane 50
Barton Hey Drive 60
Baskervyle Road 62
Bayswater Road 35
Beach Road 53
Beacon Drive 59
Beaconsfield Close 14
Beatrice Avenue 23
Beatty Close 60
Beaumaris Road 35
Bedford Road 14
Ben Nevis Road 18
Beresford Avenue 22
Berrylands Road 50
Bidston Village Road 29
Birchfield 52
Birchwood Avenue 7
Birchwood Close 7
Birkdale Drive 27
Birkenhead Road 55
Birket Avenue 47
Birket Close 47
Birket Square 47
Bolton Road 24
Borough Road (Birkenhead) 8
Borough Road (Seacombe) 44
Boswell Road 18
Boyd Close 49
Braemore Road 33
Bramble Way 50
Brassey Street 9
Breck Road 33

67

Breckside Avenue 33
Brecon Road 19
Brenig Street 13
Brian Avenue 63
Bridgecroft Road 40
Bridge Road 58
Brisbane Avenue 37
Broadfield Avenue 30
Bromborough Village Road 26
Brookhurst Avenue 28
Broster Avenue 51
Broster Close 51
Brotherton Close 26
Brougham Avenue 14
Brougham Road 44
Brow Lane 61
Browning Avenue 15
Bulwer Street 16
Burns Avenue 41
Buxton Lane 34
Byerley Street 44
Canning Street 6
Carrington Road 41
Castle Close 47
Castle Drive 61
Castleford Rise 47
Castlegrange Close 47
Castleheath Close 47
Castle Road 40
Castleway North 47
Castleway South 47
Cavendish Road 7
Cavendish Street 7
Cedar Street 7
Celtic Road 55
Central Park Avenue 39
Centurion Close 55
Centurion Drive 55
Chamberlain Street 46
Cheltenham Crescent 47
Chester Street 6
Chetwynd Road 16
Cheviot Road 19

Childwall Avenue 51
Chiltern Road 19
China Farm Lane 59
Christchurch Road 10
Church Close 42
Church Crescent 45
Church Drive 24
Churchill Grove 43
Church Lane (Thurstaston) 64
Church Lane (Woodchurch) 31
Churchmeadow Road 42
Church Road (Bebington) 21
Church Road (Thornton Hough) 63
Church Road (Upton) 30
Church Road (Wallasey) 45
Church Road (West Kirby) 57
Church Street (Birkenhead) 5
Church Street (Wallasey) 42
Church Walk 57
Clare Crescent 34
Claremount Road 34
Clarence Road 45
Clarendon Road 42
Clare Way 34
Cleveland Street 5
Clydesdale Road 54
Cobden Avenue 15
Coleridge Drive 23
Collingwood Road 22
Columbus Drive 63
Column Road 59
Common Field Road 31
Coningsby Drive 41
Connaught Close 13
Connaught Way 13
Conway Street 7
Coppice Grange 52
Cornelius Drive 63
Corniche Road 24
Cornwall Drive 17
Corona Road 25
Cotswold Road 19
Cottage Drive East 62

Cottage Drive West 62
Cottage Lane 62
Cowdrey Avenue 30
Cranbourne Avenue 51
Cressida Avenue 23
Cromarty Road 33
Cromer Road 54
Cunard Avenue 43
Cunningham Close 60
Curlew Way 51
Curzon Road 17
Curzon Road (Hoylake) 54
Dalmorton Road 36
Danger Lane 50
Dee Lane 57
Dee View Road 61
Demesne Street 44
Devonshire Road 8
Dickens Aveue 17
Dickens Close 17
Domville Drive 31
Douglas Road 59
Douglas Street 7
Dovedale Road 54
Dovepoint Road 56
Downham Drive 61
Downham Road North 61
Downham Road South 61
Drake Road 48
Duck Pond Lane 17
Duncan Street 7
Dundonald Street 11
Durban Road 41
Earlston Road 39
Edgebaston Way 29
Edgewood Road 56
Edinburgh Drive 17
Edward Road 54
Egbert Road 56
Egerton Road 23
Egerton Wharf 8
Eleanor Road 30
Eliot Close 23

Epsom Drive 47
Epsom Road 47
Erfurt Avenue 22
Ethelbert Road 56
Etna Street 14
Everest Road 18
Exmouth Street 10
Fairfax Road 11
Fairhaven Drive 27
Fairview Avenue 40
Farmfield Drive 30
Farmside 48
Farr Hall Drive 61
Farr Hall Road 61
Felicity Grove 50
Ferndale Road 54
Ferry Road 28
Forest Close 56
Forest Road 56
Fort Street 42
Forwood Road 26
Fowell Road 36
Franklin Road 49
Friars Close 21
Frobisher Road 48
Garden Lane 50
Gardenside 48
Garrick Road 18
Gautby Road 16
Gayton Mill Close 62
George Road 54
Gibson Close 64
Gladstone Close 12
Gladstone Hall Road 25
Glasier Road 51
Gleggside 59
Glencoe Road 41
Goldsmith Road 18
Goodwood Drive 47
Grammar School Lane 59
Grange Mount 5
Grange Road (Birkenhead) 5
Grange Road (West Kirby) 57

Grange Road West 5
Grass Wood Road 31
Green Lane 47
Grenville Drive 63
Griffin Avenue 50
Hamilton Square 6
Hamilton Street 6
Hampden Road 11
Harcourt Street 12
Hardie Avenue 51
Harrison Drive 34
Harrow Road 34
Hartington Avenue 12
Harvest Lane 50
Heatherdene Road 58
High Street 26
Hill Bark Road 32
Hillside Road (Wallasey) 33
Hillside Road (Heswall) 62
Hillview Avenue 58
Hinderton Road 8
Holland Road 41
Holm Hill 58
Home Farm Road 31
Homestead Mews 58
Horatio Street 10
Hose Side Road 35
Hospital Road 25
Hoylake Road 50
Hoyle Road 53
Hudson Road 49
Humber Street 13
Hurst Bank 15
Hydro Avenue 57
Ikin Close 30
Ilchester Road 8
Imperial Road 41
Ingestre Road 16
Ingleborough Road 19
Inman Road 30
Irvine Road 18
Ismay Avenue 43
Ivy Street 6

James Street 45
Jellicoe Close 60
Johnson Road 18
Jubilee Crescent 25
Juliet Avenue 23
Kimberley Road 41
King Edward Drive 25
King George's Drive 25
Kings Drive 60
Kingsmead Road 48
King's Parade 38
Kingston Close 50
King Street 42
Kipling Avenue 16
Kirket Lane 21
Kirkway 40
Knox Street 5
Laird Street 6
Lake Road 53
Larchwood Drive 21
Larkin Close 24
Leasoweside 48
Legh Road 23
Leigh Road 57
Leopold Street 45
Lester Drive 64
Lighthouse Road 53
Lillie Close 30
Limbo Lane 64
Limekiln Lane 46
Lindwall Close 30
Lingham Close 50
Lingham Lane 50
Livingstone Road 50
Livingstone Street 12
Longfellow Drive 23
Longview Avenue 40
Lords Avenue 29
Loretto Road 34
Lowwood Road 7
Luke Street 45
Lytton Avenue 16
Macdona Drive 58

Macdonald Road 51
Mackenzie Road 49
Maddock Road 39
Magazine Avenue 41
Magazine Brow 41
Magazine Lane 41
Magazine Road 27
Mainwaring Road (Bromborough) 26
Mainwaring Road (Wallasey) 44
Mallaby Street 9
Mallard Way 51
Mallory Road 18
Malvern Grove 19
Manor Drive 31
Manor Hill 16
Manor Lane 39
Manor Road (Liscard) 39
Manor Road (Thornton Hough) 63
Maple Street 7
Market Street 6
Mark Rake 27
Mark Street 45
Marlborough Road 43
Marmion Road 55
Marsden Close 42
Marshfield Court 47
Maryland Lane 50
Masefield Close 24
Matthew Street 45
Mayer Avenue 21
Meadow Crescent 31
Meddowcroft Road 39
Melbourne Street 37
Mendip Road 19
Methuen Street 11
Mill Hill 17
Mill Hill Road 64
Millhouse Lane 51
Mill Lane (Heswall) 62
Mill Lane (Liscard) 39
Mill Road 65
Millthwaite Road 33
Milner Street 11

Miranda Avenue 23
Molyneux Drive 38
Monk Road 40
Monks Ferry 6
Monks Way (Bebington) 21
Monks Way (West Kirby) 58
Montpellier Crescent 37
Morpeth Wharf 8
Mosslands Drive 34
Mount Pleasant Road 39
Mount Road 39
Murrayfield Drive 48
Nantwich Close 31
Naples Road 45
Nelson Drive 63
Nelson Street 42
Newbury Way 47
New Chester Road 8
Newell Road 40
Newland Drive 34
Newport Avenue 35
New Tower Court 38
Normanston Close 17
Normanston Road 17
North Drive 38
North Parade 53
Oakdale Avenue 44
Oakdale Road 44
Oaklands Drive 22
Oarside Drive 39
Observatory Road 29
Old Chester Road 8
Oldfield Close 62
Oldfield Drive 62
Oldfield Farm Lane 62
Oldfield Road 62
Oldfield Way 62
Old Hall Road 26
Old Mill Close 62
Old Pump Lane 32
Orchard Grange 52
Osborne Avenue 43
Palmerston Street 12

Park Road East 7
Park Road North 7
Park Road South 7
Park Road West 7
Parkside 39
Parkside Road 21
Park Street 39
Pasture Road 50
Peel Avenue 14
Pendennis Road 42
Penkett Road 39
Pennine Road (Birkenhead) 19
Pennine Road (Wallasey) 33
Pensby Road 63
Peter Street 45
Pleasant Road 39
Plumer Street 11
Poet's Corner 25
Pool Lane 26
Portal Mews 64
Portal Road 64
Portia Avenue 23
Poulton Road 45
Poulton Hall Road 45
Prenton Farm Road 17
Prenton Hall Road 17
Price Street 5
Priory Street 5
Priory Road 58
Priory Wharf 5
Pullman Close 62
Pump Lane 32
Quarry Lane 65
Queen Mary's Drive 25
Queen's Drive 17
Queen's Road 54
Radley Road 34
Rake Lane 39
Rakersfield Court 38
Rakersfield Road 38
Rappart Road 44
Ravenswood Avenue 15
Rectory Road 57

Redcar Road 35
Redcap Close 35
Reeds Avenue 48
Reeds Lane 48
Reservoir Road 13
Ribble Street 13
Richmond Street 37
Riverbank Close 62
Riverbank Road 62
Riverside 57
Robin Way 32
Rocklands Avenue 21
Rock Park 14
Rock Park Road 14
Rolleston Drive 34
Roman Road 55
Rosalind Avenue 23
Roscote Close 61
Rosebery Avenue 17
Rosebery Grove 42
Ross Avenue 49
Rowson Street 36
Royden Avenue 43
Rugby Road 34
Rundle Street 11
Ruskin Avenue 15
Russell Road 14
St Aidans Court 9
St Albans Road 40
St Andrews Road 21
St Anne Street 9
St Annes Grove 9
St Annes Place 9
St Annes Way 9
St Bridgets Lane 57
St George's Way 63
St Hilary Brow 33
St Hilary Drive 33
St James Road (Birkenhead) 10
St James Road (New Brighton) 36
St Johns Close 55
St Johns Road 42
St Johns Sqaure 9

St Johns Street 9
St Mary's Avenue 40
St Mary's Street 40
St Nicholas Road 34
St Oswalds Avenue 29
St Pauls Avenue 45
St Pauls Road 45
St Peters Close 61
St Peters Road 14
St Stephens Road 9
St Vincent Street 10
St Werburghs Square 9
Salacre Close 31
Salacre Crescent 31
Salacre Lane 31
Saltburn Road 35
Sandcliffe Road 35
Sandiways Road 35
Sandringham Avenue 54
Sandringham Drive 37
Sandy Lane (Wallasey) 35
Sandy Lane (West Kirby) 57
Sandymount Road 35
Saxon Road 56
School Hill 61
School Lane (Bidston) 29
School Lane (Meols) 55
School Lane (Thurstaston) 65
School Lane (Wallasey) 35
Seabank Road (Liscard) 39
Seabank Road (Heswall) 62
Seaview Avenue 40
Seaview Road 40
Sedbergh Road 34
Serpentine Road 39
Severn Street 13
Seymour Street 38
Shackleton Road 49
Shakespeare Avenue 15
Shakespeare Street 45
Shannon Sreet 13
Shaw Lane 32
Sheen Road 40

Shelley Way 58
Sherborne Road 34
Sherlock Lane 46
Shrewsbury Road (Birkenhead) 16
Shrewsbury Road (Wallasey) 35
Slessor Avenue 59
Smithy Hill 63
Smugglers Way 35
Snowden Road 51
Snowdon Road 18
Solway Street 13
Sparks Lane 65
Spenser Avenue 15
Stanhope Drive 27
Stanley Lane 28
Stanley Road 53
Statham Road 30
Station Road (Heswall) 61
Station Road (Hoylake) 54
Station Road (Thurstaston) 65
Steel Road 40
Stonehouse Road 34
Stoneleigh Grove 15
Strand Road 53
Strathcona Road 41
Strathearn Road 61
Sudworth Road 36
Sumner Road 10
Sunningdale Drive 27
Tancred Road 41
Tees Street 13
Tennyson Avenue 15
Tern Way 51
The Causeway 25
The Cedars 52
The Glade 56
The Green 26
The King's Gap 53
The Kirklands 58
The Laund 34
The Mount 61
The Paddock 52
The Rake 26

The Ridgeway 62
The Roscote 61
The Sandhills 47
The Woodlands 7
Thorneycroft Street 11
Tobin Street 42
Tollemache Road 16
Townfield Way 39
Town Meadow Lane 50
Townsend Street 9
Trafalgar Avenue 42
Trafalgar Drive 22
Trafalgar Road 42
Trent Street 13
Trinity Road 54
Trinity Street 9
Troon Close 27
Troutbeck Close 31
Trueman Close 30
Turret Road 40
Tweed Street 13
Twickenham Drive 48
Tyne Street 13
Unicorn Way 20
Upper Brassey Street 9
Uppingham Road 35
Urmson Road 39
Venables Close 26
Venables Drive 26
Vicarage Close 9
Victoria Avenue 61
Victoria Drive 58
Victoria Parade 37
Victoria Park Road 13
Victoria Road (Birkenhead) 13
Victoria Road (New Brighton) 37
Victoria Road (West Kirby) 58
Victoria Street 25
Village Road 57
Vittoria Street 10
Vyner Close 29
Vyner Road North 29
Vyner Road South 29

Wallasey Bridge Road 8
Walmsley Street 43
Warren Road 54
Washbrook Avenue 30
Waterloo Place 10
Waterloo Road 37
Waterpark Road 17
Water Street 25
Waverley Road 55
Webster Avenue 43
Wellesley Grove 22
Wellington Close 22
Wellington Road (Bebington) 22
Wellington Road (New Brighton) 37
Well Lane (Greasby) 32
Well Lane (Heswall) 62
Wentworth Drive 27
Wetstone Lane 58
Wharf Street 25
Wheatland Lane 44
Wilfred Owen Drive 16
Winchester Road 34
Windsor Street 37
Winser Street 25
Winston Grove 51
Withensfield 40
Withens Lane 40
Wittering Lane 62
Woburn Place 14
Wood Close 7
Woodcote Bank 15
Woodland Avenue 56
Woodland Grove 15
Woodland Road 56
Wood Street 7
Wordsworth Avenue 15
Wordsworth Walk 58
Wright Street 43
Yew Tree Close 31
York Avenue 58
York Road 45
York Street 26
Zig Zag Road 40